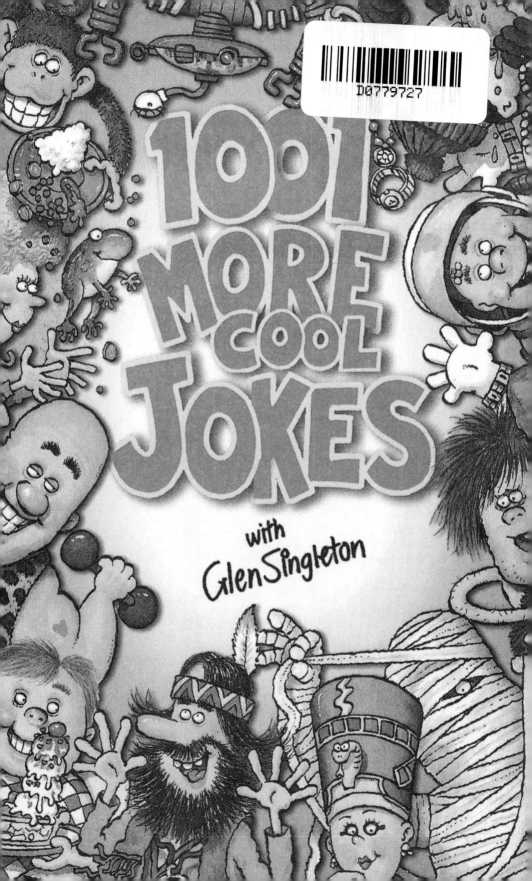

1001 MORE COOL JOKES

with
Glen Singleton

1001 More Cool Jokes
First published in 2003 by
Hinkler Books Pty Ltd
17–23 Redwood Drive
Dingley VIC 3172 Australia
www.hinklerbooks.com

© Hinkler Books Pty Ltd 2002

Reprinted 2003

Publisher's thanks to Barb Whiter for compiling the jokes.
Cover design & illustrations by Glen Singleton.

ISBN: 1 865 15 960 3

Printed and bound in Australia

CONTENTS

Animals   4

Computers   25

Dinosaurs   28

Doctor Doctor   30

Jokes about Boys   45

Jokes about Girls   66

Knock Knock   91

Miscellaneous   106

Monsters, Witches,
Ghosts, and Vampires   112

Riddles   131

School   142

Silly Book Titles   161

Space   178

Sport   182

Crazy Fools   190

What do you call . . . ?   195

Wicked   198

Animals

1 **W**hat is a polygon?
A dead parrot.

2 **W**hat do owls sing when it's raining?
Too wet to woo.

3 **W**hat has 500 pairs of sneakers, a ball, and two hoops?
A centipede basketball team.

Obviously a very rich elephant who chose not to eat his peanuts

4 **W**hy do elephants never get rich?
Because they work for peanuts.

AAHRRR

AARRRR

5 **W**hat is striped and bouncy?
A tiger on a pogo stick.

6 **W**hen do kangaroos celebrate their birthdays?

During leap year.

7 **W**hat did one bee say to her nosy neighbor bee?

"Mind your own bees' nest!"

8 **W**hat do you do with a mouse that squeaks?

You oil him.

9 **W**ho was the first deer astronaut?

Buck Rogers.

10 **W**here does a pig go to pawn his watch?

A ham hock shop.

11 **W**hat happens when a chimpanzee sprains his ankle?

He gets a monkey wrench.

12 **W**hat happened to the male bee that fell in love?

He got stuck on his honey.

13 **W**hat flies through the jungle singing operetta?

The parrots of Penzance.

14 **W**hat's the best way to catch a monkey?

Climb a tree and act like a banana.

15 **W**hat do you get if you cross a tiger with a sheep?

A striped sweater.

16 **W**hat do you get if you cross a tiger with a snowman?

Frostbite.

17 **W**hat do you get if you cross a tiger with a kangaroo?

A striped jumper.

18 **W**hat is white, lives in the Himalayas and lays eggs?

The Abominable Snow Chicken.

19 **W**hat do you call a crazy chicken?

A cuckoo cluck.

20 **W**hat do you get if you cross Bambi with a ghost?

Bamboo.

21 **O**n which side does an eagle have most of its feathers?

On the outside.

22 **W**hat do you call a crate of ducks?

A box of quackers.

23 **W**hat's the difference between a mouse and an elephant?

About a ton.

The luckiest bug in the pond

24 **W**hat happened to two frogs that caught the same bug at the same time?

They got tongue-tied.

25 **W**hat's the best way to face a timid mouse?

Lie down in front of its mouse hole and cover your nose with cheese spread!

26 **W**hat do termites eat for dessert?

Toothpicks.

Do you like your toothpicks with a slice of salami and a cocktail onion?

No... I prefer mine plain!

27 **W**hat time is it when an elephant climbs into your bed?

Time to get a new bed.

MUM! Has the elephant been in my bedroom again?

28 **W**hat kind of key doesn't unlock any doors?

A donkey.

29 **W**hat do you get if you cross a hyena with a bouillon cube?

An animal that makes a laughing stock of itself.

30 **W**hat do you get if you pour hot water down a rabbit hole?

Hot cross bunnies.

31 **W**hy did the man cross a chicken with an octopus?

So everyone in his family could have a leg each.

Now... if the striped sausages are ZEBRA...then the spotted ones must be LEOPARD. So then...what are the plain ones?

32 **W**hat has six legs and can fly long distances?

Three swallows.

33 **W**hat do you get if you cross a pig with a zebra?

Striped sausages.

34   **W**hat do vultures always have for dinner?
Leftovers.

35   **W**hat do you get if you cross a duck with a firework?
A fire-quacker.

36   **W**hat do patriotic monkeys wave on July 4th?
Star spangled bananas.

37   **W**hy do buffaloes always travel in herds?
Because they're afraid of getting mugged by elephants.

38   **W**here do sharks shop?
The fish market.

39   **W**hat do you call the autobiography of a shark?
A fishy story.

40 **W**hy don't baby birds smile?

Would you smile if your mother fed you worms all day?

41 **W**hat do you call a travelling mosquito?

An itch hiker.

42 **W**hat is a duck's favorite T.V. show?

The feather forecast.

43 **W**hat did the rabbit give his girlfriend when they got engaged?

A 24-carrot ring.

44 **W**hat do you do if your chicken feels sick?

Give her an eggs-ray.

45 **W**hat sort of music is played most in the jungle?

Snake, rattle, and roll.

46 **W**here do tadpoles change into frogs?

The croakroom.

47 **W**hat's the tallest yellow flower in the world?

A giraffodil.

48 **W**hat do elephants take when they can't sleep?

Trunkquilisers.

49 **W**hich animals were the last to leave the ark?

The elephants – they were packing their trunks.

50 **H**ow do ducks play tennis?

With a quacket.

51 **W**hat sort of a bird steals from banks?

A robin.

52 **W**hy do bears have fur coats?

Because they can't get plastic raincoats in their size!

53 **W**hat would you get if you crossed a hunting dog with a journalist?

A news hound.

54 **W**here is the hottest place in the jungle?

Under a gorilla.

55 **W**hat do you call a bull taking a nap?

A bull dozer.

56 **W**hat is the biggest ant in the world?

An eleph-ant.

57 **W**hat's even bigger than that?

A gi-ant!

58 **H**ow many ants are needed to fill an apartment?

Ten-ants.

59 **W**here do ants eat?

A restaur-ant.

60 **W**hat bird is always out of breath?

A puffin.

61 **W**hat's the difference between a gym teacher and a duck?

One goes quick on its legs and the other goes quack on its legs!

62 **H**ow do fireflies start a race?

Ready, set, glow!

63 **W**hat do you get if you cross a leopard with a watchdog?

A terrified postman.

64 **W**hy were flies playing football in a saucer?

They were playing for the cup.

65 **W**hat do you get if you cross a bottle of water with an electric eel?

A bit of a shock!

66 **W**hat do you get if you cross an eel with a shopper?

A crazy customer.

67 **W**hat do you call a neurotic octopus?

A crazy, mixed-up squid.

68 **W**hat do you call a bird that lives underground?

A mynah bird.

69 **W**hich birds steal the soap from the bath?

Robber ducks.

70 **H**ow do we know that owls are smarter than chickens?

Have you ever heard of Kentucky-fried owl?

71 **W**hat do tigers wear in bed?

Striped pajamas!

72 **W**hen is a lion not a lion?

When he turns into his den.

73 **W**hat does an octopus wear when it's cold?

A coat of arms.

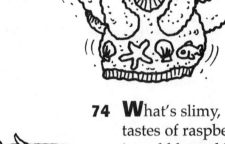

WASH DAY AT THE OCTOPUS' PLACE

What flavor jelly have you got? I've got raspberry!

I think mine's Lime by the feel of it!

74 **W**hat's slimy, tastes of raspberry, is wobbly and lives in the sea?

A red jellyfish.

75 **W**hat is a parrot's favorite game?

Hide and speak.

76 **W**hat do parrots eat?

Polyfilla.

GOOD STUFF?

MMMMM M-M-M...MM MMMMMM!

POLYFILLA

77 What do you call a Scottish parrot?

A Macaw.

78 What do you get if you cross a parrot with a shark?

A bird that will talk your ear off!

79 What do you get if you cross an electric eel with a sponge?

Shock absorbers.

80 What's an eel's favorite song?

"Slip Sliding Away."

81 What do you get if you cross a frog with a small dog?

A croaker spaniel.

82 What is a narrow squeak?

A thin mouse!

83 **W**hat's small, squeaks, and hangs out in caves?

Stalagmice.

84 **W**hat do you call a mouse that can pick up a monster?

Sir.

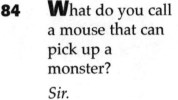

85 **W**hat happens when ducks fly upside-down?

They quack up.

86 **H**ow can you tell the difference between a rabbit and a monster?

Ever tried getting a monster into a rabbit hutch?

87 **W**hat happened when the owl lost his voice?

He didn't give a hoot.

88 **W**hat goes "dot, dot, dash, squeak?"

Mouse code.

An owl with laryngitis

89 **W**hat do you get if you cross a parrot with a woodpecker?

A bird that talks in Morse code.

90 **I**f you cross a witch's cat with Father Christmas, what do you get?

Santa Claws.

91 **N**ow you see it, now you don't. What could you be looking at?

A black cat walking over a zebra crossing!

92 **W**hat do you call a deer with no eyes?

No idea.

93 **W**here do Noah's bees live?

In ark hives.

94 **W**hat's another name for a clever duck?

A wise quacker!

95 **W**hat is a termite's favorite breakfast?

Oak-meal.

96 **W**hat's the difference between a mosquito and a fly?

Try zipping up a mosquito!

97 **W**hy did the insects drop the centipede from their football team?

He took too long to put on his shoes!

98 **W**hat did the lion say to his cubs when he taught them to hunt?

Don't walk across the road until you see the zebra crossing.

99 **W**hat do lions say before they go out hunting for food?

Let us prey.

100 **W**hat flies around your light at night and can bite off your head?

A tiger moth.

101 **W**hat's a lion's favorite food?

Baked beings.

102 **W**hat does a lion brush his mane with?

A catacomb.

103 **W**hat happened when the lion ate the comedian?

He felt funny.

104 **H**ow can you get a set of teeth put in for free?

Tease a lion.

105 **H**ow does a lion say hi! to other animals?

Pleased to eat you!

106 **W**hat's the difference between a tiger and a lion?

A tiger has the mane part missing.

107 **W**hat happened to the leopard who took four baths every day?

Within a week he was spotless.

108 **W**hy are tigers and sergeants in the army alike?

They both wear the stripes.

109 **W**hy did the lion feel sick after he'd eaten the priest?

Because it's hard to keep a good man down.

110 **W**hat do you call a lion wearing a hat?

A dandy lion.

111 **W**hat did the lioness say to the cub chasing the hunter?

Stop playing with your food.

112 **W**hat did the croaking frog say to her friend?

I think I've got a person in my throat.

113 **W**hat did the termite say when she saw that her friends had completely eaten a chair?

Wooden you know it!

Computers

114 **H**ow do computers make sweaters?

On the interknit.

115 **W**hy was the computer in pain?

It had a slipped disk!

YOUCH! I've slipped a disc. Someone call a CHIROPRACTOR!

116 **W**hy was the computer so thin?

Because it hadn't had many bytes!

117 **W**hy did the cat sit on the computer?

To keep an eye on the mouse.

The cat that made off with the mouse...and the computer

118 What sits in the middle of the world wide web?

A very, very big spider.

119 Why did the vampire bite a computer?

Because he wanted to get on the interneck.

120 "Do you turn on your computer with your left hand or your right hand?"

"My right hand."

"Amazing! Most people have to use the on/off switch!"

121 "Is this the computer help line?

Every time I log on as a Seven Dwarf, my computer screen goes snow white."

122 Customer: "I cleaned my computer, and now it doesn't work."

Repairman: *"What did you clean it with?"*

Customer: "Soap and water."

Repairman: *"Water's not meant to be used on a computer!"*

Customer: "Oh, I bet it wasn't the water that caused the problem. It was when I put it in the dryer!"

123 **D**id you hear about the monkey who left bits of his lunch all over the computer?

His dad went bananas.

124 **H**ow do you stop your laptop batteries from running out?

Hide their sneakers!

125 **"I** bought this computer yesterday and I found a twig in the disk drive!"

"I'm sorry, Sir. You'll have to speak to the branch manager."

126 **"I**'ve been on my computer all night!"

"Don't you think you'd be more comfortable on a bed, like everyone else?"

127 **"M**om, Mom, Dad's broken my computer!"

"How did he do that?"

"I dropped it on his head!"

Dinosaurs

128 **W**hy do dinosaurs have wrinkles in their knees?

Because they've stayed in the bath too long.

129 **W**hy did the dinosaur fall out of a palm tree?

Because a hippopotamus pushed him out.

130 **W**hat do you get if you cross a dinosaur with a werewolf?

Who knows, but I wouldn't want to be within a thousand miles of it when the moon is full!

131 **W**hy do dinosaurs have flat feet?

Because they don't wear sneakers.

132 **H**ow do you tell if a dinosaur comes to visit?

He parks his tricycle outside.

133 **W**hy did the dinosaur lie on his back in the water and stick his feet up?

So people could see he wasn't a bar of soap.

134 **W**hy do dinosaurs wear glasses?

So they don't step on other dinosaurs.

135 **W**hat's red on the outside and green inside?

A dinosaur wearing red pajamas.

136 **W**hat do you get if you cross a dinosaur with a kangaroo?

A huge animal that causes earthquakes wherever it hops.

137 **W**hat do you get if you cross a dinosaur with a termite?

A huge bug that eats big buildings for breakfast!

Doctor, Doctor

138 **D**octor, Doctor, I have a carrot growing out of my ear.

Amazing! How could that have happened?

I don't understand it. I planted cabbages in there!

139 **D**octor, Doctor, I've spent so long at my computer that I now see double.

Well, walk around with one eye shut.

140 **D**octor, Doctor, can I have a bottle of aspirin and a pot of glue?

Why?

Because I've got a splitting headache!

141 **D**octor, Doctor, my little brother thinks he's a computer.

Well bring him in so I can cure him.

I can't. I need to use him to finish my homework!

142 **D**octor, Doctor, should I surf the Internet on an empty stomach?

No, you should do it on a computer.

143 **D**octor, Doctor, my girlfriend thinks she's a duck.

You'd better bring her in to see my right away.

I can't. She's already flown south for the winter.

144 **D**octor, Doctor, I think I've been bitten by a vampire.

Drink this glass of water.

Will it make me better?

No, but I'll be able to see if your neck leaks!

145 **D**octor, Doctor, my son has swallowed my pen. What should I do?

Use a pencil until I get there.

146 **D**octor, Doctor, I think I'm a bell.

Take these, and if they don't help, give me a ring!

147 **D**octor, Doctor, I've got gas! Can you give me something?

Yes! Here's my car.

148 **D**octor, Doctor, I keep thinking I'm a dog.

Sit on the couch and we'll talk about it.

But I'm not allowed on the furniture!

149 **D**octor, Doctor, I think I'm a bridge.

What's come over you?

Oh, two cars, a large truck, and a bus.

150 Doctor, Doctor, can I have a second opinion?

Of course, come back tomorrow.

151 Doctor, Doctor, when I press with my finger here . . .

it hurts, and here . . .

it hurts, and here . . .

and here!

What do you think is wrong with me?

Your finger's broken!

152 Doctor, Doctor, you have to help me out!

That's easy. Which way did you come in?

153 Doctor, Doctor, I've swallowed my harmonica!

Well, it's a good thing you don't play the piano.

154 Doctor, Doctor, I keep getting a pain in the eye when I drink coffee.

Have you tried taking the spoon out of the cup before you drink?

155 **D**octor, Doctor, I feel like a spoon!
Well, sit down and don't stir!

156 **D**octor, Doctor, I think
I need glasses.
You certainly do. You've just walked into a restaurant!

157 **D**octor, Doctor, I've just swallowed a pen.
Well, sit down and write your name!

158 **D**octor, Doctor, I feel like a dog.
Sit!

159 **D**octor, Doctor, I feel like an apple.
We must get to the core of this!

160 **D**octor, Doctor, I feel like a sheep.
That's baaaaaaaaaad!

161 **D**octor, Doctor, I'm becoming invisible.

Yes, I can see you're not all there!

162 **D**octor, Doctor, will this ointment clear up my spots?

I never make rash promises!

163 **D**octor, Doctor, everyone keeps throwing me in the garbage.

Don't talk rubbish!

164 **D**octor, Doctor, I'm boiling up!

Just simmer down!

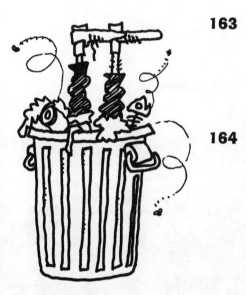

165 **D**octor, Doctor, I feel like a needle.

I see your point!

166 **D**octor, Doctor, how can I cure my sleepwalking?

Sprinkle thumb tacks on your bedroom floor!

A GUARANTEED CURE FOR SLEEPWALKING

167 **D**octor, Doctor, I feel like a racehorse.

Take one of these every four laps!

168 **D**octor, Doctor, I feel like a bee.

Buzz off. I'm busy!

169 **D**octor, Doctor, I'm a burglar!

Have you taken anything for it?

170 **D**octor, Doctor, I keep seeing an insect spinning.
Don't worry. It's just a bug that's going around.

171 **D**octor, Doctor, how can I stop my nose from running?
Stick your foot out and trip it up!

172 **D**octor, Doctor, I'm having trouble with my breathing.
I'll give you something that will soon put a stop to that!

173 **D**octor, Doctor, I tend to flush a lot.
Don't worry. It's just a chain reaction.

174 **D**octor, Doctor, everyone thinks I'm a liar.
Well, that's hard to believe!

175 **D**octor, Doctor, my baby looks just like his father.
Never mind – just as long as he's healthy.

176 Doctor, Doctor, what did the x-ray of my head show?

Absolutely nothing!

177 Doctor, Doctor, I think I'm a python.

You can't get around me that easy, you know!

178 Doctor, Doctor, I keep thinking I'm a mosquito.

Go away, sucker!

179 Doctor, Doctor, I think I'm a moth.

So why did you come around then?

Well, I saw this light at the window . . .

180 Doctor, Doctor, I think I'm a moth.

Get out of the way. You're in my light!

181 Doctor, Doctor, I keep thinking I'm a spider.

What a web of lies!

182 Doctor, Doctor, I think I'm a snail.

Don't worry. We'll soon have you out of your shell.

183 Doctor, Doctor, I think I'm a calculator.

Great, can you help me with my accounts please?

184 Doctor, Doctor, I keep painting myself gold.

Don't worry. It's just a gilt complex.

185 Doctor, Doctor, I think I'm a rubber band.

Why don't you stretch yourself out on the couch there, and tell me all about it?

186 Doctor, Doctor, I feel like a pair of curtains.

Oh, pull yourself together!

187 Doctor, Doctor, everyone keeps ignoring me.

Next please!

188 Doctor, Doctor, I keep thinking I'm a computer.

My goodness, you'd better come to my office right away!

I can't. My power cable won't reach that far!

189 Doctor, Doctor, I don't think I'm a computer any more.

Now I think I'm a desk.

You're just letting things get on top of you.

190 Doctor, Doctor, I think I'm a computer.

How long have you felt like this?

Ever since I was switched on!

191 Doctor, Doctor, I keep thinking there's two of me.

One at a time please!

192 Doctor, Doctor, some days I feel like a tipi and other days I feel like a wigwam.

Relax, you're too tents!

193 Doctor, Doctor, my little boy has just swallowed a roll of film.

Hmmm. Let's hope nothing develops!

194 Doctor, Doctor, I can't get to sleep.

Sit on the edge of the bed, and you'll soon drop off.

195 Doctor, Doctor, I feel like a pack of cards.

I'll deal with you later!

196 Doctor, Doctor, I snore so loudly that I keep myself awake.

Sleep in another room, then.

197 Doctor, Doctor, I have a split personality.

Well, you'd better both sit down, then.

198 Doctor, Doctor, my sister keeps thinking she's invisible.

Which sister?

199 Doctor, Doctor, I think I'm a yo-yo.

You're stringing me along!

200 Doctor, Doctor, I keep thinking I'm a vampire.

Necks, please!

201 Doctor, Doctor, I swallowed a bone.

Are you choking?

No, I really did!

202 Doctor, Doctor, I dream there are zombies under my bed. What can I do?

Saw the legs off your bed.

203 Doctor, Doctor, I think I'm a drill.

How boring for you!

204 **D**octor, Doctor, I think I'm an electric eel.

That's shocking!

205 **D**octor, Doctor, I think I'm a nit.

Will you get out of my hair?

Some patients just get in your hair

206 **D**octor, Doctor, I've broken my arm in two places.

Well, don't go back there again.

207 **D**octor, Doctor, I think I'm a butterfly.

Will you say what you mean and stop flitting about!

208 **D**octor, Doctor, I think I'm a frog.

What's wrong with that?

I think I'm going to croak!

CROAK

Oh that's better!

209 Doctor, Doctor, I think I'm a caterpillar.

Don't worry. You'll soon change.

210 Doctor, Doctor, my hair keeps falling out. Can you give me something to keep it in?

Sure, here's a paper bag.

211 Doctor, Doctor, these pills you gave me for B.O . . .

What's wrong with them?

They keep slipping out from under my arms!

212 Doctor, Doctor, my husband smells like a fish.

Poor sole!

213 Doctor, Doctor, my sister thinks she's an elevator.

Well tell her to come in.

I can't, she doesn't stop at this floor!

Jokes about Boys

214 **M**om: *"Why are you scratching Jamie?"*
Jamie: *"Because no one else knows where I itch.*

215 **D**id you hear about the boy who wanted to run away to the circus?
He ended up in a flea circus!

216 **W**hy did the boy take an aspirin after hearing the werewolf howl?
Because it gave him an eerie ache.

217 **D**id you hear about the boy who saw a witch riding on a broomstick?

He asked *"What are you doing on that?"*

She replied *"My sister has the vacuum cleaner!"*

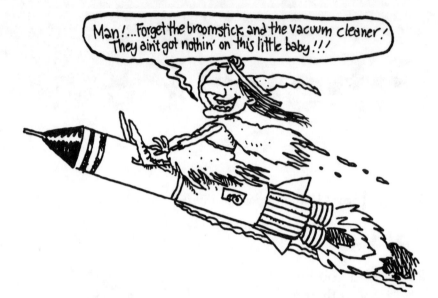

218 **A** little boy came running into the kitchen.

"Dad, Dad" he said, *"there's a monster at the door with a really ugly face."*

"Tell him you've already got one," said his father!

219 **W**hy was the boy
unhappy to win the
prize for best costume
at the Halloween
party?

*Because he just came to
pick up his little sister!*

220 **W**hy did the boy
carry a clock and a
bird on Halloween?

It was for tick or tweet!

A few too many good turns I feel

221 **D**id you hear about the
dizzy Boy Scout?

*He spent all day doing good
turns.*

222 **B**oy monster: *"You have a
face like a million dollars."*

Girl monster: *"Have I really?"*

Boy monster: *"Sure, it's
green and wrinkly!"*

223 **W**hat do you get if
you cross a zombie
with a Boy Scout?

*A creature that scares
old ladies across the
street.*

224 **H**ow did the invisible boy upset his mother?

He kept appearing.

225 **I**gor: *"How was that horror movie you saw last night?"*

Dr. Frankenstein: *"Oh, the same old story: Boy meets girl, boy loses girl, boy builds new girl."*

226 **D**id you hear about the boy who got worried when his nose grew to be 11 inches long?

He thought it might turn into a foot.

227 **D**id you hear about the little boy who was named after his father?

They called him Dad.

228 **D**id you hear about the two boys who found themselves in a modern art gallery by mistake?

"Quick," said one. *"Run, before they say we did it!"*

229 **A** boy broke his arm playing football.

After his arm had been put into a cast, he asked the doctor, *"When you take the plaster off, will I be able to play the drums?"*

"Of course you will," said the doctor, reassuringly.

"That's great!" said the boy. *"I've never been able to play before!"*

230 **R**oy: *"They say ignorance is bliss."*

Rita: *"Then you should be the happiest boy in the world!"*

231 **"K**eep that dog out of my garden. It's disgusting!"* a neighbor said to a little boy one day.

The boy went home to his family and told them to stay away from the neighbor's garden because of the bad smell!

232 **D**id you hear about the boy who sat under a cow?

He got a pat on the head.

233 **D**id you hear about the boy who was known as Fog?

He was dense and wet!

234 **B**oys' favorite films

The Fly, Batman, Beetlejuice, The Sting, The Good, The Bug and the Ugly, Spawn, The Frog Prince, Four Webbings and a Funeral, Seven Bats for Seven Brothers.

235 **W**hy did the boy take a pencil to bed?

To draw the curtains!

236 **I**'d tell you another joke about a boy and a pencil, but there's no point.

237 **W**hy did the lazy boy get a job in a bakery?

Because he wanted to loaf around!

238 **A** naughty boy was annoying all the passengers on a plane.

At last, one man could stand it no longer.

"Hey kid," he shouted. *"Why don't you go outside and play?"*

239 **J**ack: *"Mom, all the boys at school call me Big Head."*

Mom: *"Never mind, Dear. Just run down to the grocery store and bring home the big bag of apples in your baseball hat."*

240 **G**ood news: Two boys went out to climb trees.

Bad news: *One of them fell out.*

Good news: A hammock was beneath him.

Bad news: *A rake was beside the hammock.*

Good news: He missed the rake.

Bad news: *He missed the hammock too!*

241 **W**hy did the boy wear five watches?

He liked to have a lot of time on his hands.

242 **D**id you hear about the boy who stole some rhubarb?

He was put into custardy.

243 **T**wo boys camping out in the backyard wanted to know the time, so they started singing at the top of their voices.

Soon, one of the neighbors threw open his window and shouted, *"Hey, cut the noise! Don't you know it's 3 o'clock in the morning?"*

244 **W**hen George left school he was going to be a printer.

All his teachers said he was the right type.

245 A boy staying in an old house meets a ghost in the middle of the night.

"I've been walking these corridors for 300 years," says the ghost.

"In that case, can you tell me where the bathroom is?" asks the boy.

246 A little boy came home from his first day at kindergarten and said to his mother, *"What's the use of going to school? I can't read, I can't write, and the teacher won't let me talk!"*

247 Did you hear about the boy who had to do a project about trains?

He had to keep track of everything.

248 Mother: *"Who was that on the phone, Sammy?"*

Sammy: *"No one we knew, Mom. Just some man who said it was long distance from Australia, so I told him I knew that already!"*

249 A scoutmaster asked a boy in his troop what good deed he had done that day.

"Well," said the Scout. *"My Mom only had one chore left, so I let my brother do it.'*

250 Charlie had a puppy on a leash. He met his brother Jim and said,

"I just got this puppy for our little brother."

"Really?" said Jim. *"That was a good trade!"*

251 First boy: *"My brother said he'd tell me everything he knows."*

Second boy: *"He must have been speechless!"*

252 First boy: *"Why is your brother always flying off the handle?"*

Second Boy: *"Because he has a screw loose!"*

253 Peter: *"My brother wants to work badly!"*

Anita: *"As I remember, he usually does!"*

254 Dan: *"My little brother is a real pain."*

Nan: *"Things could be worse."*

Dan: *"How?"*

Nan: *"He could be twins!"*

255 First boy: *"Does your brother keep himself clean?"*

Second boy: *"Oh, yes. He takes a bath every month, whether he needs one or not!"*

256 Mom: *"What are you doing, Son?"*

Boy: *"Writing my brother a letter."*

Mom: *"That's a nice idea, but why are you writing so slowly?"*

Boy: *"Because he can't read very fast!"*

257 Little brother: *"I'm going to buy a seahorse."*

Big brother: *"Why?"*

Little brother: *"Because I want to play water polo!"*

258 Big brother: *"That planet over there is Mars."*

Little brother: *"Then that other one must be Pa's."*

259 Why did your brother ask your father to sit in the freezer?

Because he wanted an ice pop!

260 Why did the boy wear a life jacket in bed?

Because he slept on a waterbed.

261 **"M**y brother's a professional boxer."

"Heavyweight?"

"No, featherweight. He tickles his opponents to death!"

Feather weight's secret weapon

262 Dad: *"Don't be selfish. Let your brother use the sled half the time."*

Son: *"I do, Dad. I use it going down the hill, and he gets to use it coming up the hill!"*

263 **W**hy did your brother go to school at night?

Because he wanted to learn to read in the dark!

264 **D**id you hear about my brother?

He saw a moose's head hanging on a wall and went into the next room to find the rest of it!

265 **M**om: *"Why does your little brother jump up and down before taking his medicine?"*

Boy: *"Because he read the label and it said, 'shake well before using'."*

266 **"M**y brother's been practicing the violin for ten years."

"Is he any good?"

"No, it was nine years before he found out he wasn't supposed to blow!"

267 **L**ittle brother: *"Look, Bro, I have a deck of cards."*

Big brother: *"Big deal!"*

268 My big brother is such a fool. The other day I saw him hitting himself over the head with a hammer.

He was trying to make his head swell so his hat wouldn't fall over his eyes!

269 Was the carpenter's son a chip off the old block?

270 Dad: *"Why is your January progress report so bad?"*

Son: *"Well, you know how it is. Things are always marked down after Christmas!"*

271 Will and Bill were arguing about whose father was stronger.

Will said, *"Well, you know the Pacific Ocean? My dad dug the hole for it."*

Bill wasn't impressed.

"Well, that's nothing. You know the Dead Sea? My father's the one who killed it!"

272 **A** man whose son had just passed his driving test came home one evening and found that the boy had driven into the living room.

"How did you manage that?" he fumed.

"Quite simple, Dad," said the boy. *"I just came in through the kitchen and turned left."*

273 **M**om: *"Haven't you finished filling the salt shaker yet?"*

Son: *"Not yet. It's really hard to get the salt through all those little holes!"*

274 **F**irst witch: *"I took my son to the zoo yesterday."*

Second witch: *"Really? Did they keep him?"*

275 **"W**hy are you crying, Ted?" asked his mom.

"Because my new sneakers hurt," Ted replied.

"That's because you've put them on the wrong feet."

"But they're the only feet I have!"

276 **N**ed: *"What does your dad sell?"*

Ed: *"Salt."*

Ned: *"Well, my dad is a salt seller too."*

Ed: *"Shake!"*

277 "Mom, can I please change my name right now?" asked Ben.

"Why would you want to do that, Dear?" asked his mom.

"Because Dad says he's going to spank me, as sure as my name's Benjamin!"

ABNER ....
ADELBERT ....
AETHELRED ...
ALGERNON ...
ALONZO ...
ARCHIBALD ..

A-Z of BABY NAMES

278 Did you hear about the farmer's boy who hated the country?

He went to the big city and got a job as a shoeshine boy, and so the farmer made hay while the son shone.

LOOK..! NO CAKE!

279 "William," shouted his Mom. "There were two pieces of cake in that pantry last night, and now there's only one. How do you explain that?"

"It was dark in the pantry," said William. "And I didn't see the second piece!"

280 Charley: *"My cat likes to drink lemonade."*

Lenny: *"He sure must be a sourpuss!"*

281 Did you hear what Dumb Donald did when he offered to paint the garage for his dad?

The instructions said put on three coats, so he put on his jacket, his raincoat, and his overcoat!

282 Dad was taking Danny around the museum when they came a cross a magnificent stuffed lion in a case.

"Dad," asked a puzzled Danny.

"How did they shoot the lion without breaking the glass?"

283 Dick and Jane were arguing over the breakfast table.

"Oh, you're so stupid!" shouted Dick.

"Dick!" said their father.

"That's quite enough! Now say you're sorry."

"Okay," said Dick. *"Jane, I'm sorry you're stupid."*

284 Mom: *"How can you practice your trumpet and listen to the radio at the same time?"*

Son: *"Easy, I have two ears!"*

285 **"I** *think my Dad's getting taller,"* said Stan, to his friend.

"What makes you think that?"

"Well, lately I've noticed that his head is sticking through his hair."

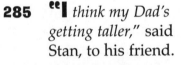

286 **J**ohnny collected lots of money from trick-or-treating and he went to the store to buy some chocolate.

"You should give that money to charity," said the shopkeeper.

"No thanks," replied Johnny. *"I'll buy the chocolate. You give the money to charity!"*

287 **"W**illiam, I've been told you're fighting with the boys next door," said his dad.

"Yes Dad," said William. "They're twins, and I needed a way to tell them apart!"

288 **O**ne day Joe's mother said to his father,

"It's such a nice day, I think I'll take Joe to the zoo."

"I wouldn't bother," said his father.

"If they want him, let them come and get him!"

289 **G**eorge knocked on the door of his friend's house.

When his friend's mother answered he asked, "Can Albert come out to play?"

"No," said Albert's mother. "It's too cold."

"Well, then," said George. "Can his soccer ball come out to play?"

290 **B**oy: "Grandpa, do you know how to croak?"

Grandpa: "No, I don't. Why?"

Boy: "Because Daddy says he'll be a rich man when you do!"

291 **W**hy did Matt's bicycle keep falling over?

Because it was two tired.

292 **"M**om," Richard yelled, from the kitchen.

"You know that vase you were always worried I'd break?"

"Yes, Dear. What about it?" asked his mom.

"Well . . . your worries are over."

Mom won't be too mad.... It's only broken into 3 big bits

293 **W**hen Dad came home, he was amazed to see his son sitting on a horse, writing something.

"What are you doing up there?" he asked.

"Well, the teacher told us to write an essay on our favorite animal," replied the boy.

294 **"M**om, there's a man at the door collecting for the old folk's home," said the little boy.

"Shall I give him Grandma?"

295 **"T**he girl who sits beside me in math is very clever," said Alec, to his mother.

"She has enough brains for two."

"Perhaps you'd better think of marriage," said his mom.

296 **A** young boy was helping his dad around the house.

"Son, you're like lightning with that hammer," said the father.

"Really fast, eh, Dad?" said the boy.

"No, Son. You never strike in the same place twice!"

Jokes about Girls

297 **W**hat happened when the girl dressed as a spoon left the Halloween party?

No one moved. They couldn't stir without her.

298 **F**irst witch: *"My, hasn't your little girl grown!"*

Second witch: *"Yes, she's certainly gruesome."*

You've grown up into the ugliest most gruesome daughter a Mom could ever want!

299 **T**wo girls were having lunch in the schoolyard.

One had an apple, and the other said, *"Watch out for worms!"*

The first girl replied, *"Why should I? They can watch out for themselves!"*

300 **S**ally: *"Can I try on that dress in the window?"*

Salesgirl: *"If you like, but most people use the dressing room."*

301 **T**eacher: *"I'd like you to be very quiet today, girls. I've got a dreadful headache."*

Mary: *"Why don't you do what my mom does when she has a headache?"*

Teacher: *"What's that?"*

Mary: *"She sends us out to play!"*

302 **G**irl: *"Do you like me?"*

Boy: *"As girls go, your fine — and the sooner you go, the better!"*

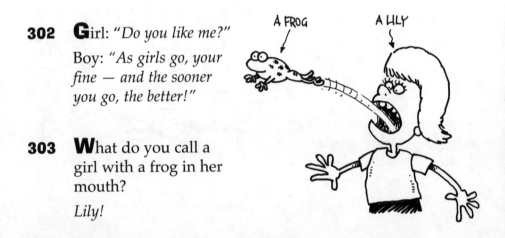

A FROG

A LILY

303 **W**hat do you call a girl with a frog in her mouth?

Lily!

304 **H**ow does a witch doctor ask a girl to dance?

"Voodoo like to dance with me?"

My... you do have short legs... It feels like I'm dragging you along...

You are!

305 **G**irl: *"I'd buy that dog, but his legs are too short."*

Salesgirl: *"Not really. All four of them touch the floor."*

306 **W**hy did the wizard turn the naughty girl into a mouse?

Because she ratted on him.

307 **W**hat kind of girl does a Mummy take on a date?

Any old girl he can dig up.

308 **F**irst monster: *"That pretty girl over there just rolled her eyes at me."*

Second monster: *"Well, you'd better roll them back. She might need them!"*

309 **W**hat happened to the girl who wore a mouse costume to the Halloween party?

The cat ate her.

310 **S**ome girls who are the picture of health are just painted that way.

311 **W**ho is a vampire likely to fall in love with?

The girl necks door.

312 **T**wo girls were talking in the corridor.

"That boy over there is getting on my nerves," said Clare.

"But he's not even looking at you," replied Megan.

"That's why he's getting on my nerves!" exclaimed Clare.

313 **"A**lice, you never get anything right,"* complained the teacher.

"What kind of job do you think you'll get when you leave school?"

"Well, I want to be a weather girl on T.V." said Alice.

314 **D**id you hear about the girl monster who wasn't pretty and wasn't ugly?

She was pretty ugly!

315 First cannibal: *"Who was that girl I saw you with last night?"*

Second cannibal: *"That was no girl. That was my dinner."*

316 What did the Eskimo schoolboy say to the Eskimo schoolgirl?

What's an ice girl like you doing in a place like this?

317 First girl: *"Whenever I'm down in the dumps, I buy myself a new hat."*

Second girl: *"Oh, so that's where you get them!"*

318 "Those raisin cookies you sold me yesterday had three cockroaches in them," a girl complained over the phone, to the baker.

"Sorry about that," said the baker.

"If you bring the cockroaches back, I'll give you the three raisins I owe you."

319 Why did the girl take a load of hay to bed?

To feed her nightmare.

320 What is a myth?

A female moth!

321 What do young female monsters do at parties?

They go around looking for edible bachelors!

322 **H**ave you met the girl who wanted to marry a ghost?

I can't think what possessed her!

323 **W**hy did the small werewolf bite the girl's ankle?

Because he couldn't reach any higher.

324 **A** girl walked into a pet shop and said, *"I'd like a frog for my brother."*

"Sorry," said the shopkeeper. *"We don't do exchanges!"*

325 **D**id you hear about the girl who was so hung up on road safety that she always wore white at night?

Last winter she was knocked down by a snow plow.

326 **D**id you hear about the girl who got engaged and then found out her new fiancé had a wooden leg?

She broke it off, of course.

327 **F**ather: *"I want to take my girl out of this terrible math class."*

Teacher: *"But she's top of the class!"*

Father: *"That's why it must be a terrible class!"*

328 **H**andsome Harry: *"Every time I walk past a girl, she sighs."*

Wisecracking William: *"With relief!"*

329 **W**hy was the Egyptian girl worried?

Because her daddy was a mummy!

330 **B**ill: *"My sister has lovely long hair, all down her back."*

Will: *"Pity it's not on her head!"*

331 **W**hat do you call an amorous insect?

A love bug!

73

332 **H**ow did the octopus couple walk down the road?

Arm in arm, in arm, in arm, in arm, in arm, in arm, in arm, in arm ...

333 **W**hat do girl snakes write on the bottom of their letters?

With love and hisses!

334 **W**itch: *"When I'm old and ugly, will you still love me?"*

Wizard: *"I do, don't I?"*

335 **W**hat happened when the young wizard met the young witch?

It was love at first fright.

336 **D**id you hear about the vampire who died of a broken heart?

She had loved in vein.

337 **W**hy did the girl cut a hole in her new umbrella?

Because she wanted to tell when it stopped raining!

338 **M**other: *"Why did you put a toad in your brother's bed?"*

Daughter: *"Because I couldn't find a spider."*

So what am I supposed to do now? Hop about wildly all night with a couple of stinky feet?

339 **W**hy did the girl separate the thread from the needle?

Because the needle had something in its eye.

340 **W**hy did the girl wear a wet shirt all day?

Because the label said "wash and wear".

341 **W**hy did the girl spend two weeks in a revolving door?

Because she was looking for the doorknob.

342 **D**id you hear about the girl who wrote herself a letter but forgot to sign it?

When it arrived, she didn't know who it was from!

343 Brother: *"What happened to you?"*

Sister: *"I fell off while I was riding."*

Brother: *"Horseback?"*

Sister: *"I don't know. I'll find out when I get back to the stable."*

344 **F**irst girl: *"Why are you putting your horse's saddle on backward?"*

Second girl: *"How do you know which way I'm going?"*

345 **W**hy doesn't your sister like peanuts?

Have you ever seen a skinny elephant?

346 **W**hat kind of sharks never eat women?

Man-eating sharks!

347 **W**hy did the girl feed money to her cow?

Because she wanted to get rich milk.

348 **W**hy did the girl tiptoe past the medicine cabinet?

Because she didn't want to wake the sleeping pills.

349 **M**y sister went on a crash diet.

Is that why she looks a wreck?

350 **W**hy didn't the girl want tickets for a door prize?

Because she already had a door.

351 **W**hy did the girl give cough syrup to the pony?

Because someone told her it was a little horse.

352 **W**hy did the girl have yeast and shoe polish for breakfast?

Because she wanted to rise and shine in the morning!

353 **B**rother: *"Did you just take a shower?"*

Sister: *"Why, is one missing?"*

354 **W**hy did your sister keep running around her bed?

Because she was trying to catch up with her sleep!

355 **M**ary: *"Do you think my sister's pretty?"*

Gary: *"Well, let's just say if you pulled her pigtail, she'd probably say 'oink, oink'!"*

356 Why was your sister fired from her job as an elevator operator?

Because she couldn't remember the route.

357 Did you hear about the girl who got her brother a birthday cake but then couldn't figure out how to get the cake in the typewriter to write 'Happy Birthday'?

358 Why did the girl plant birdseed?

Because she wanted to raise canaries!

359 Why did your sister put her socks on inside out?

Because there was a hole on the outside.

360 My sister is so dim that she thinks a cartoon is something you sing in the car!

361 First vampire: *"I don't think much of your sister's neck!"*

Second vampire: *"Don't worry. Just eat the vegetables."*

362 **D**id you hear about the time Eddie's sister tried to make a birthday cake?

The candles melted in the oven.

363 **W**hy did the girl jump out of the window?

Because she wanted to try out her new spring suit.

364 **W**hy did the girl take a bicycle to bed?

Because she didn't want to walk in her sleep.

365 **W**hat do you call the cannibal who ate her father's sister?

An aunt-eater!

366 **W**hy did the girl put a chicken in a tub of hot water?

Because she wanted the chicken to lay hard-boiled eggs!

367 **L**ucy: *"If you eat any more ice cream, you'll burst."*

Lindy: *"Okay. Pass the ice cream and duck."*

368 **M**other: *"Cathy, get your little sister's hat out of that puddle!"*

Cathy: *"I can't, Mom. She's got it strapped too tight under her chin."*

369 **J**anet: *"What's the difference between a cake and a school bus?"*

Jill: *"I don't know."*

Janet: *"I'm glad I didn't send you to pick up my birthday cake!"*

370 **M**y sister is so dumb that she thinks a buttress is a female goat!

371 **B**oy: *"Dad! Dad! Come out! My sister's fighting a 10-foot gargoyle with three heads!"*

Dad: *"No, I'm not coming out. She's going to have to learn to look after herself."*

372 **F**irst man: *"My girlfriend eats like a bird."*

Second man: *"You mean she hardly eats a thing?"*

First man: *"No, she eats slugs and worms."*

373 **T**wo cannibals were having lunch.

"Your girlfriend makes a great soup," said one to the other.

"Yes!" agreed the first. *"But I'm going to miss her!"*

374 **F**irst cannibal: *"My girlfriend's a tough old bird."*

Second cannibal: *"You should have left her in the oven for another half-hour."*

375 **"D**o you think, Professor, that my girlfriend should take up the piano as a career?"

"No, I think she should put down the lid as a favor!"

376 **J**ames: *"I call my girlfriend Peach."*

John: *"Because she's soft and beautiful as a peach?"*

James: *"No, because she's got a heart of stone."*

377 **W**hen Wally Witherspoon proposed to his girlfriend, she said,

"I love the simple things in life, but I don't want one of them for a husband!"

378 **"I** got a gold watch for my girlfriend."

"I wish I could make a trade like that!"

379 **"I**t's a pity you've gone on a hunger strike," said the convict's girlfriend on visiting day.

"Why?" asked the convict.

"Because I've put a file in your cake!"

380 "My girlfriend says that if I don't give up golf, she'll leave me."

"Say, that's tough, man."

"Yeah, I'm going to miss her."

381 What did the wizard say to his witch girlfriend?

Hello, gore-juice!

382 My girlfriend talks so much that when she goes on vacation, she has to spread suntan lotion on her tongue!

383 What did the skeleton say to his girlfriend?

I love every bone in your body!

384 **W**hat did the undertaker say to his girlfriend?

Em-balmy about you!

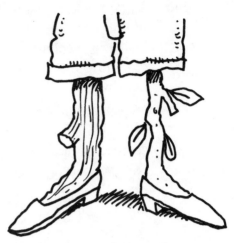

385 **I** can't understand why people say my girlfriend's legs look like matchsticks.

They do look like sticks, but they certainly don't match!

386 **E**very time I take my girlfriend out for a meal, she eats her head off.

She looks better that way.

Oh...
I can't wear
these socks out
tonight...
They've got a
hole in them!

387 **E**mma: *"What a cool pair of odd socks you have on, Jill."*

Jill: *"Yes, and I have another pair just like it at home."*

388 **B**rother: *"Where was Solomon's temple?"*

Sister: *"On either side of his head."*

389 **K**ate: *"I'm going to cross a galaxy with a frog."*

Sharon: *"You'll be sorry. Don't you know what you'll get?"*

Kate: *"No. What?"*

Sharon: *"Star warts!"*

390 Little Susie stood in the department store near the escalator, watching the moving handrail.

"Something wrong, little girl?" asked the security guard.

"Nope," replied Susie. "I'm just waiting for my chewing gum to come back."

391 Girl: "How much is a soft drink?"
Waitress: "Fifty cents."
Girl: "How much is a refill?"
Waitress: "The first is free."
Girl: "Well, then, I'll have a refill."

392 Maria: "Whatever will Tammy do when she leaves school?

She's not smart enough to get a job!"

Bonnie: "She could always be a ventriloquist's dummy."

393 Teacher: "Sue, what letter comes after the letter A?"

Sue: "The rest of them."

394 "**M**ary," said her teacher. *"You can't bring that lamb into class. What about the smell?"*

"Oh, that's all right," replied Mary. *"It'll soon get used to it."*

395 **W**hy did Silly Sue throw her guitar away?

Because it had a hole in the middle.

396 **V**isitor: *"You're very quiet, Louise."*

Louise: *"Well, my mom gave me a dollar not to say anything about your red nose."*

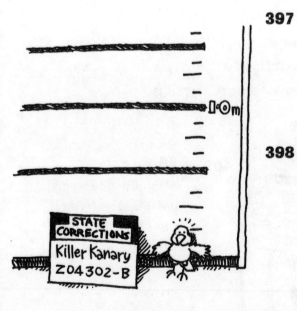

397 **B**iology teacher: *"What kind of birds do we keep in captivity?"*

Janet: *"Jail birds!"*

398 **J**ane: *"Do you ever do any gardening?"*

Wayne: *"Not often. Why?"*

Jane: *"You look as if you could use some remedial weeding."*

399   Mary: *"I've a soft spot for you."*

Harry: *"Ah, really?"*

Mary: *"Yes, in the middle of a swamp!"*

400   "What shall we play today?" Tanya asked her best friend, Emma.

"Let's play school," said Emma.

"Okay," said Tanya. "But I'm going to be absent."

401   Helen: *"Mom, do you know what I'm going to give you for your birthday?"*

Mom: *"No, Dear. What?"*

Helen: *"A nice teapot."*

Mom: *"But I already have a nice teapot."*

Helen: *"Not anymore. I just dropped it!"*

402   Mom: *"Jill, go and play with your whistle outside. Your father can't read his paper."*

Jill: *"Wow, I'm only 8 and I can read it."*

403 Mary's class went to the Natural History Museum.

"Did you enjoy yourself?" asked her mother, when she got home.

"Oh, yes," replied Mary. *"But it was funny going to a dead zoo!"*

404 **"M**rs Johnston, your daughter would be a fine dancer, except for two things."

"What are they?"

"Both feet!"

405 Jane was telling her friend about her vacation in Switzerland. Her friend asked, *"What did you think of the beautiful scenery?"*

"Oh, I couldn't see much," said Jane.

"There were too many mountains in the way."

89

406   Girl to friend: *"I'm sorry, I won't be able to come out tonight. I promised Dad I'd stay in and help him with my homework."*

407   *"I hope this plane doesn't travel faster than sound,"* said the girl to the flight attendant.

"Why?" asked the flight attendant.

"Because my friend and I want to talk, that's why!"

408   Penny: *"Will you join me in a cup of hot chocolate?"*

Mindy: *"Yes, but do you think we'll both fit?"*

Knock, Knock.

409 **K**nock, Knock.
Who's there?
Abba!
Abba who?
Abba banana!

410 **K**nock, Knock.
Who's there?
Abbey!
Abbey who?
Abbey stung me on the nose!

411 **K**nock, Knock.
Who's there?
Abbott!
Abbott who?
Abbott time you opened this door!

412 **K**nock, Knock.
Who's there?
Abe!
Abe who?
Abe C D E F G H . . .

413 **K**nock, Knock.
Who's there?
Abel!
Abel who?
Abel seaman!

414 **K**nock, Knock.
Who's there?
Abyssinia!
Abyssina who?
Abyssinia when I get back!

415 **K**nock, Knock.
Who's there?
Adair!
Adair who?
Adair once, but I'm bald now!

416 **K**nock, Knock.
Who's there?
Adam!
Adam who?
Adam up and tell me the total!

417 **K**nock, Knock.

Who's there?

Arthur!

Arthur who?

Arthur any more at home like you!

418 **K**nock, Knock.

Who's there?

Baby Owl!

Baby Owl who?

Baby Owl see you later, maybe I won't!

419 **K**nock, Knock.

Who's there?

Bach!

Bach who?

Bach of chips!

420 **K**nock, Knock.

Who's there?

Bacon!

Bacon who?

Bacon a cake for your birthday!

421 **K**nock, Knock.
Who's there?
Barbara!
Barbara who?
Barbara black sheep, have you any wool!

422 **K**nock, Knock.
Who's there?
Bernadette!
Bernadette who?
Bernadette my lunch and now I'm starving!

423 **K**nock, Knock.
Who's there?
Olive!
Olive who?
Olive you!

424 **K**nock, knock.
Who's there?
Bee!
Bee who?
Bee careful!

425 **K**nock, Knock.
Who's there?
Beef!
Beef who?
Bee fair now!

426 **K**nock, Knock.
Who's there?
Bella!
Bella who?
Bella bottom trousers!

427 **K**nock, Knock.
Who's there?
Ben!
Ben who?
Ben away a long time!

428 **K**nock, Knock.
Who's there?
Biafra!
Biafra who?
Biafra'id, be very afraid!

429 **K**nock, Knock.
Who's there?
Boxer!
Boxer who?
Boxer tricks!

430 **K**nock, Knock.
Who's there?
Bowl!
Bowl who?
Bowl me over!

431 **K**nock, Knock.
Who's there?
Bridie!
Bridie who?
Bridie light of the
silvery moon!

432 **K**nock, Knock.
Who's there?
Brie!
Brie who?
Brie me my supper!

433 **K**nock, Knock.

Who's there?

Butcher!

Butcher who?

Butcher arms around me!

434 **K**nock, Knock.

Who's there?

Butcher!

Butcher who?

Butcher left leg in, your left leg out!

BUTCHER LEFT LEG IN AND SHAKE IT ALL ABOUT

435 **K**nock, Knock.

Who's there?

Butcher!

Butcher who?

Butcher money where your mouth is!

436 **K**nock, Knock.

Who's there?

C-2!

C-2 who?

C-2 it that you don't forget my name next time!

437 **K**nock, Knock.
Who's there?
Caesar!
Caesar who?
Caesar quickly, before she gets away!

438 **K**nock, Knock.
Who's there?
Caesar!
Caesar who?
Caesar jolly good fellow!

439 **K**nock, Knock.
Who's there?
Carlotta!
Carlotta who?
Carlotta trouble when it breaks down!

440 **K**nock, Knock.
Who's there?
Cantaloupe!
Cantaloupe who?
Cantaloupe with you tonight!

441 **K**nock, Knock.
Who's there?
Canoe!
Canoe who?
Canoe come out
and play with
me?

442 **K**nock, Knock.
Who's there?
Carmen!
Carmen who?
Carmen get it!

443 **K**nock, Knock.
Who's there?
Carol!
Carol who?
Carol go if you turn the ignition key!

444 **K**nock, Knock.
Who's there?
Cows!
Cows who?
Cows go
"moo", not
"who"!

445 **K**nock, Knock.
Who's there?
Quacker!
Quacker who?
Quacker 'nother bad joke and I'm leaving!

446 **K**nock, Knock.
Who's there?
Nobody!
Nobody who?
Just nobody!

447 **K**nock, Knock.
Who's there?
U-2!
U-2 who?
U-2 can buy a brand new car for only $199 a month!

448 **K**nock, Knock.
Who's there?
U-4!
U-4 who?
U-4 me and me for you!

449 **K**nock, Knock.
Who's there?
U-8!
U-8 who?
U-8 my lunch!

450 **K**nock, Knock.
Who's there?
Utah!
Utah who?
Utah the rails and I'll mend the fence!

451 **K**nock, Knock.
Who's there?
Zany!
Zany who?
Zany body home?

452 **K**nock, Knock.
Who's there?
Zeke!
Zeke who?
Zeke and you shall find!

453 **K**nock, Knock.
Who's there?
Zubin!
Zubin who?
Zubin eating garlic again!

454 **K**nock, Knock.
Who's there?
X!
X who?
X-tremely pleased to meet you!

455 **K**nock, Knock.
Who's there?
X!
X who?
X for breakfast!

456 **K**nock, Knock.
Who's there?
Xavier!
Xavier who?
Xavier money for a rainy day!

457 **K**nock, Knock.
Who's there?
Xavier!
Xavier who?
Xavier breath, I'm not leaving!

458 **K**nock, Knock.
Who's there?
Xena!
Xena who?
Xena minute!

459 **K**nock, Knock.
Who's there?
Xenia!
Xenia who?
Xenia stealing my candy!

460 **K**nock, Knock.
Who's there?
Jam!
Jam who?
Jam mind, I'm trying to get out!

461 **K**nock, Knock.
Who's there?
James!
James who?
James people play!

462 **K**nock, Knock.
Who's there?
Jaws!
Jaws who?
Jaws truly!

463 **K**nock, Knock.
Who's there?
Jilly!
Jilly who?
Jilly out here, so
let me in!

464 **K**nock, Knock.
Who's there?
Jim!
Jim who?
Jim mind if we
come in!

465 **K**nock, Knock.
Who's there?
Jimmy!
Jimmy who?
Jimmy a little kiss on the cheek!

466 **K**nock, Knock.
Who's there?
Gable!
Gable who?
Gable to leap tall buildings in a single bound!

467 **K**nock, Knock.
Who's there?
Jo!
Jo who?
Jo jump in the lake!

468 **K**nock, Knock.
Who's there?
Gary!
Gary who?
Gary on smiling!

Just a happy guy

469 **K**nock, Knock.
Who's there?
Gizza!
Gizza who?
Gizza kiss!

kissy kissy kissy

Miscellaneous

470 **"S**o you are distantly related to the family next door, are you?"

"Yes. Their dog is our dog's brother."

471 **"C**harley, why did Farley run through the screen door?" asked Mom.

"Because he wanted to strain himself!"

472 **H**ow do you make a potato puff?

Chase it around the garden.

473 **W**hat vegetable goes well with jacket potatoes?

Button mushrooms.

474 **W**hat jam can't you eat?

A traffic jam!

475 **I**f the Mounties always get their man, what do postmen always get?

Their mail.

476 Why are giraffes good friends to have?

Because they stick their neck out for you.

477 **W**hat do you get when you cross an orange with a squash court?

Orange squash.

478 **"C**an you lend me $1000?"

"I only have $800."

"That's okay. You can owe me the other $200."

479 **S**tatistics say that one in three people is mentally ill.

So check your friends and if two of them seem okay, you're the one.

480 Amy: *"Did you find your cat?"*

Karen: *"Yes, he was in the refrigerator."*

Amy: *"Goodness, is he okay?"*

Karen: *"Yes, he's cool!"*

481 **W**hat do you get if you cross a worm with a baby goat?

A dirty kid.

482 **W**hy was the glowworm unhappy?

Her children weren't very bright.

483 **W**hat's the hottest letter in the alphabet?

It's 'b', because it makes oil boil!

484 **W**hat's the difference between Santa Claus and a warm dog?

Santa wears the suit, but a dog just pants.

485 **W**hy did the farmer plow his field with a steamroller?

He wanted to grow mashed potatoes.

486 **W**e went for a holiday last year to a seaside town.

It was so boring there that the tide went out one day and didn't come back!

487 **W**hat do bees do if they need a ride?

Wait at a buzz stop.

488 **W**hat's green and short and goes camping?

A boy sprout.

489 What's the difference between a night watchman and a butcher?

One stays awake and the other weighs a steak!

490 What's green, covered in custard, and sad?

Apple grumble.

491 **W**hat happened when there was a fight in the seafood restaurant?

Two fish got battered.

492 **W**hat's the difference between a young lady and a fresh loaf?

One is a well-bred maid and the other is well-made bread.

Where all the slow tomatoes end up.

493 **W**hat did one tomato say to the one behind him?

Ketchup!

494 **D**uck: "Do you have any lip gloss?"

Storekeeper: *"Yes, of course. Will that be cash or credit?"*

Duck: *"Just put it on my bill."*

Would you like it on your bill?

No... on the credit card thanks!

Monsters, Witches, Ghosts and Vampires

495 **W**hat do you get if you cross Frankenstein with a hot dog?

Frankenfurterstein.

496 **W**hat monster is the most untidy?

The Loch Mess Monster.

Well, it's definitely been here.... Just look at the mess!

VIEW THE LOCH MESS MONSTER HERE

497 **W**hat do you call a monster airline steward?

A fright attendant.

498 **W**hy did the monster buy an ax?

Because he wanted to get ahead in life.

499 **W**hat is a monster's favorite game?

Hide and Shriek.

500 **W**hat do Italian monsters eat?

Spookgetti.

501 **W**hat do Hungarian monsters eat?

Ghoulash.

502 **W**hat should you take if a monster invites you to dinner?

Someone who can't run as fast as you.

503 **W**hat do you think when you see a monster?

"I hope he hasn't seen me!"

504 **W**hat do you do with a blue monster?

Try to cheer him up a bit.

505 **W**hy did the monster comedian like playing to skeletons?

Because he knew how to tickle their funny bones.

506 **W**hat do you call a monster that comes to collect your laundry?

An undie-taker.

507 **I**f you crossed the Loch Ness monster with a shark, what would you get?

Loch Jaws.

508 **W**hat eats its victims two by two?

Noah's Shark.

509 **H**ow do you talk to
the Loch Ness
monster when he's
so far under water?

Drop him a line.

510 **D**uring which age
did Mummies live?

The Band-Age.

511 **W**hy was the monster catching centipedes?

He wanted scrambled legs for breakfast.

512 **W**hat does a ghost call his Mom and Dad?

His transparents.

513 **H**ow does Frankenstein eat?

He bolts his food down.

514 **W**hat's a good job for a young monster?

Chop assistant.

515 **W**hat did the metal monster want on his gravestone?

Rust in Peace.

516 **W**here do skeletons keep their money?

In a joint account.

517 **W**hy didn't the skeleton and the monster fight?

The skeleton didn't have the guts.

518 **H**ow many monsters would it take to fill your living room?

How would I know? I'd leave as soon as the first one arrived!

519 **W**hat do you do if a monster rolls his eyes at you?

Just pick them up and roll them back!

520 **W**hy did the young monster take a runner to school in his lunch?

Because he liked fast food.

521 **W**hat do monsters make with cars?
Traffic jam.

522 **W**ho patrols cemeteries at night?
A fright watchman.

523 **W**hat do you have to buy if you invite monsters around for a party?
A new house.

SPOOKY!

Spooky TIE DIE KIT

524 **W**hat is a monster's favorite craft?
Tie and die.

525 **W**here do ghosts go to learn to frighten people?
Swooniversity.

526 **W**hat do ghosts use to type letters?
A type-frighter.

527 **W**hat type of horses do monsters ride?
Night mares.

528 **W**hat's the difference between a monster and a cookie?

Have you ever tried to dunk a monster in your milk?

529 **W**hy can't ghosts tell lies?

You can see right through them.

530 **W**hat's a monster's favorite shape?

A vicious circle.

531 **W**hat do ghosts do to keep fit?

They hire an exercisist.

532 **W**here do monsters send their clothes for cleaning?

The dry screamers.

533 **W**hat do monsters like reading in the papers every day?

Their horror-scopes, of course!

534 **W**hat type of music do Mummies prefer?

Wrap music.

535 **W**hat do baby sea monsters play with?

Sea-saws.

536 **W**hat feature do witches love on their computers?

The spell-checker.

537 **W**hy did the ghost go to jail?

For driving without due scare and attention.

538 **W**hat does a Yeti eat for dinner?

An ice burger.

539 **W**hat do you get if you cross King Kong with a frog?

A huge gorilla that can catch a plane with its tongue!

540 **D**oes a monster need a menu while vacationing on a cruise ship?

No, just the passenger list.

541 **W**hat did the monster say when he saw a rush-hour train full of passengers?

Great! A chew-chew train!

542 **W**hy did the monster eat the lightbulb?

He wanted some light refreshment.

543 **W**hat aftershave do monsters prefer?

Brute.

544 **H**ow do you know there's a monster in your shower?

You can't close the shower curtain.

545 **W**hat should you do if a monster runs through your front door?

Run out the back door.

546 **W**hy did the young monster knit herself three socks?

She grew another foot.

547 First monster: *"I've just changed my mind."*

Second monster: *"Does it work better than the old one?"*

548 **O**n which day do monsters eat people?

Chewsday.

549 What does a monster Mommy say to her kids at dinner time?

Don't speak with someone in your mouth.

550 What's the name of a clever monster?

Frank Einstein.

551 How do you stop a charging monster?

Take away his credit card.

552 How did the monster cure his sore throat?

By gargoyling every day.

553 The police are looking for a monster with one eye.

They should use two!

554 Did you hear about the monster who sent his picture to a lonely hearts club?

They sent it back, saying they weren't that lonely.

555 Did you hear about the monster who lost all his hair in the war?

He lost it in a hair raid.

556 What happened when the ice monster ate a spicy salsa?

He blew his cool.

557 Did you hear what happened to Ray when he met the man-eating monster?

He became an ex-Ray!

558 Why did the monster paint himself in rainbow-colored stripes?

He wanted to hide in a crayon box.

559 Why was the big, hairy, two-headed monster top of the school class?

Because two heads are better than one.

560 What do ghosts do in the January sales?

Go bargain haunting.

561 Why did the monster eat his music teacher?

His Bach was worse than his bite.

562 Did you hear about the little spook who couldn't sleep at night because his brother kept telling him human stories?

563 Did the bionic monster have a brother?

No, but he had lots of trans-sisters!

564 Small monster: *"Dad, the dentist wasn't painless like he said he'd be."*

Dad monster: *"Did he hurt you?"*

Small monster: *"No, but he yelled when I bit his finger!"*

565 What did Dracula call his daughter?

Bloody Mary.

566 **W**hich of the witches' friends eats the fastest?

The goblin.

567 **H**ow does a witch make scrambled eggs?

She holds the pan and gets two friends to make the stove shake with fright.

568 **W**hat do you call a pretty and friendly witch?

A failure.

569 **W**hy do demons and ghouls get on so well?

Because demons are a ghoul's best friend.

570 **H**ow does a skeleton call his friends?

On a telebone.

571 **W**hat do you call a motorcycle belonging to a witch?

A brooooooooooom stick!

572 **W**as Dracula ever married?

No, he was a bat-chelor!

573 **W**hat do you get if you cross a vampire with Al Capone?

A fangster!

574 **W**hy are skeletons usually so calm?

Nothing gets under their skin!

I'm really more the BIKINI ON A BEACHTOWEL sort of girl myself...

575 **W**hat do vampires gamble with?

Stake money!

576 **W**hy do skeletons hate winter?

Because the cold goes right to their bones!

577 **W**hat is red, sweet, and bites people?

A jampire!

578 **W**hat do you call an old and foolish vampire?

A silly old sucker!

a silly old sucker

579 **W**hat story do little witches like to hear at bedtime?

Ghoul deluxe and the three scares!

580 **W**hy do dragons sleep during the day?

So they can fight knights!

581 **W**hat should you say when you meet a ghost?

How do you boo, Sir?

582 **W**hat did the mother ghost say to the baby ghost?

Put your boos and shocks on!

583 **W**hat would you find on a haunted beach?

A sand witch!

584 **W**hen do ghosts usually appear?

Just before someone screams!

585 **W**hat do you think of Dracula films?

Fangtastic!

586 **W**ho brings the monsters their babies?

Frankenstork!

587 **W**hy are ghosts cowards?

Because they've got no guts!

588 **W**hat do Indian ghosts sleep in?

A creepy tipi!

589 **D**id you hear about the ghouls' favorite hotel?

It had running rot and mould!

590 **W**ho speaks at the ghosts' press conference?

The spooksperson!

591 **W**hat is Count Dracula's favorite snack?

A fangfurter!

592 **W**hat do ghosts eat for breakfast?

Dreaded wheat!

593 **W**hat is a ghost's favorite dessert?

Boo-Berry pie with I-scream!

594 **W**hy are graveyards so noisy?

Because of all the coffin!

595 **W**hat do you get if you cross a ghost with a packet of chips?

Snacks that go crunch in the night!

596 **H**ow does a witch tell the time?

With a witch watch!

597 **W**hy did the witch put her broom in the washing machine?

She wanted a clean sweep!

598 **W**hat do you call two witches that share a room?

Broom mates!

599 **W**hat noise does a witch's breakfast cereal make?

Snap, cackle and pop!

Riddles

600 **W**hat dance do
hippies hate?
A square dance.

601 **W**hat can be caught
and heard, but never
seen?
A remark.

602 **W**hat part of a fish
weighs the most?
The scales.

603 **W**hat's gray and can't
see well from either end?
A donkey with its eyes shut.

604 **W**hat is bigger when it's upside down?
The number 6.

605 **W**hy don't bananas get lonely?
Because they hang around in bunches.

Man...that dance
is just so
SQUARE!
You gotta start
thinking
in
HEXAGONS,
man...
HEXAGONS

606 What's the difference between a joke and a wise guy?

One is funny, and one thinks he's funny.

607 Why did the girl keep a ruler on her newspaper?

Because she wanted to get the story straight.

608 If a woman is born in China, grows up in Australia, goes to live in America and dies in New Orleans, what is she?

Dead.

609 What do well-behaved young lambs say to their mothers?

"Thank ewe!"

610 What has a hundred limbs but cannot walk?

A tree.

611 How can you tell an undertaker?

By his grave manner.

612 What can you serve, but never eat?

A tennis ball.

613 If a horse loses its tail, where could it get another?

At a re-tail store.

614 What goes through water but doesn't get wet?

A ray of light.

615 Three men were in a boat. It capsized, but only two got their hair wet. Why?

The third man was bald!

616 What do elephants play marbles with?

Old bowling balls.

617 **W**hy do doctors wear masks when operating?

Because if they make a mistake, no one will know who did it!

618 **W**hy did the girl buy a set of tools?

Everyone said she had a screw loose.

Hmmmm... Now where did they come from?

619 **W**hy is a bride always out of luck on her wedding day?

Because she never marries the best man.

620 **W**hen Adam introduced himself to Eve, what three words did he use which read the same backward and forward?

"Madam, I'm Adam."

621 **W**hy is a ladies' belt like a garbage truck?

Because it goes around and around to gather the waist.

622 **W**hat is the difference between a hungry person and a greedy person?

One longs to eat, and the other eats too long.

623 **W**hat's the difference between an oak tree and a tight shoe?

One makes acorns, the other makes corns ache.

624 **W**hat is the best cure for dandruff?

Baldness.

625 **W**hat did the dentist say to the golfer?

"You've got a hole in one!"

626 **W**hat does every girl have that she can always count on?

Fingers.

627 **W**hen a boy falls into the water, what is the first thing he does?

Gets wet.

628 **W**hat happened when the Eskimo girl had a fight with her boyfriend?

She gave him the cold shoulder.

629 What do you call a man who doesn't have all his fingers on one hand?

Normal. You have fingers on both hands!

630 What happened to the horse that swallowed the dollar?

He bucked.

631 What did one angel say to the other angel?

Halo.

632 What does a girl look for but hopes she'll never find?

A hole in her pantyhose.

633 **W**hat trees do fortune tellers prefer?

Palms.

634 **W**hat did Cinderella say when her photos weren't ready?

"Some day my prints will come."

635 **W**hy did the Invisible Man's wife understand him so well?

Because she could see right through him.

636 **W**hy can't anyone stay angry with actors?

Because they always make up.

637 **W**hy was the mother flea so sad?

Because her children were going to the dogs.

638 **W**hy did the boy laugh after his operation?

Because the doctor put him in stitches.

639 If everyone bought a white car, what would we have?

A white carnation.

640 What is a forum?

One-um plus three-um.

Obviously radical babies

641 Why do we dress baby girls in pink and baby boys in blue?

Because babies can't dress themselves.

642 What did the burglar say to the lady who caught him stealing her silver?

"I'm at your service, ma'am."

Now that's my sort of man! "Mr. October"

643 Why did the girl tear the calendar?

Because she wanted to take a month off.

644 Why didn't the boy go to work in the wool factory?

Because he was too young to dye.

645 **W**hen is a chair like a woman's dress?

When it's satin.

646 **W**hy did the boy put his bed in the fireplace?

So he could sleep like a log.

647 **W**hen does a timid girl turn to stone?

When she becomes a little bolder (boulder)!

648 **W**hy did the boy sit on his watch?

He wanted to be on time.

649 **W**hat did Santa Claus' wife say during a thunderstorm?

"Come and look at the rain, Dear."

650 **W**hat kind of star wears sunglasses?

A movie star.

651 **W**hy are good intentions like people who faint?

They need carrying out.

652 **W**hat do you call a man who shaves 30 times a day?

A barber.

653 **"D**o these stairs take you to the third floor?"

"No, I'm afraid you'll have to walk!"

654 **W**hat did the mother sardine say to her baby when they saw a submarine?

"Don't be scared. It's only a can of people."

655 **W**hy is an island like the letter T?

Because it's in the middle of water.

656 **W**hat is the fiercest flower in the garden?

The tiger lily.

657 What is higher without the head than with it?

A pillow.

658 Who was the fastest runner in the whole world?

Adam, because he was the first in the human race.

659 What kind of song can you sing in the car?

A car tune!

660 How does a boat show its affection?

By hugging the shore.

661 When do clocks die?

When their time's up.

662 What did the buffalo say to his son when he went away on a long trip?

"Bison."

663 Can a match box?

No, but a tin can!

School

A bit of geography ...

664 What are the names of the small rivers that run into the Nile?

The juve-niles.

665 What do you know about the Dead Sea?

Dead? I didn't even know it was sick!

666 Why is the Mississippi such an unusual river?

It has four eyes and can't even see.

Gee...the Mississippi really does have four eyes!

667 Where is the English Channel?

Not sure. It's not on my T.V.

668 **W**hy does the Statue of Liberty stand in New York harbor?

Because it can't sit down.

The Statue of Liberty must have gotten tired and sat down.

669 **N**ame an animal that lives on the tundra.

A reindeer.

Name another.

Another reindeer.

I reckon I'm hot on this guy's trail!

670 **D**o you know where to find elephants?

Elephants don't need finding. They're so big they don't get lost.

671 **W**hat fur do we get from a tiger?

As fur as possible.

672 **W**hat birds are found in Portugal?

Portu-geese.

673 Name three famous poles.

North, south, and tad.

674 What do you do with crude oil?

Teach it some manners.

General

675 What do you call someone who greets you at the school door every morning?

Matt.

676 Did you hear about the student who said he couldn't write an essay about goldfish because he didn't have any waterproof ink?

677 Have you heard about the gym teacher who ran around exam rooms, hoping to jog students' memories?

678 . . . Or, the home economics teacher who had her pupils in stitches?

679 ... Or, maybe, the home economics teacher who thought Hamlet was an omelette with bacon?

680 **W**hat would you get if you crossed a teacher with a vampire?

Lots of blood tests.

681 **T**eacher: *"I hope I didn't see you copying from John's exam paper, James."*

James: *"I hope you didn't see me either!"*

682 **F**ather: *"How do you like going to school?"*

Son: *"Going and coming home are fine; it's the part in the middle I don't like!"*

683 **"O**ur teacher talks to herself in class. Does yours?"

"Yes, but she doesn't realize it. She thinks we're listening!"

684 Teacher: *"Be sure to go straight home after school."*

Student: *"I can't. I live around the corner!"*

685 Laugh, and the class laughs with you.

But you get detention alone.

686 Why did the student stand on his head?

To turn things over in his mind.

687 Student: *"Where can I find out about ducks?"*

Librarian: *"Try the ducktionary."*

688 Mother: *"I told you not to eat cake before supper."*

Son: *"But it's part of my homework, see: If you take an eighth of a cake from a whole cake, how much is left?"*

Teachers

689 Teacher: *"Why can't you answer any of my questions in class?"*

Student: *"If I could, there wouldn't be much point in me being here."*

690 Teacher: *"What came after the Stone Age and the Bronze Age?"*

Student: *"The saus-age."*

691 Teacher: *"What family does the octopus belong to?"*

Student: *"Nobody's I know."*

692 Why did the teacher wear sunglasses?

Because his students were so bright.

693 Did you hear about the cross-eyed teacher?

He couldn't control his pupils.

694 Teacher: *"What's the name of a liquid that won't freeze?"*

Student: *"Hot water."*

One of those stale old bargain buns that made its way into the teacher's lunchbox

695 Teacher: *"If I bought 100 buns for a dollar, what would each bun be?"*

Student: *"Old and stale."*

696 Teacher: *"Can anyone tell me what the Dog Star is?"*
Student: *"Lassie."*

697 Did you hear about the technology teacher who left teaching to try to make something of himself?

Now students... I'm going to turn myself into...

sub-atomic particles

698 Parent: *"In my day we didn't have computers at school to help us."*

Child: *"You mean you got your schoolwork wrong all on your own?"*

699 How do you make seven an even number?
Take off the s.

700 **D**id you hear about the math teacher who wanted to order pizza for dinner, but was divided about whether to add more cheese?

Here's your ·74 share of the entire pizza with 0·25% extra cheese!

701 **W**hat do you get if you cross a homeroom teacher and a traffic cop?

Someone who gives you 500 double yellow lines for being late.

702 **W**hat is an English teacher's favorite fruit?

The Grapes of Wrath.

*A rainy night...
A dinner party...
Salmon dip...
A Butler...
All adds up to a murder to me*

703 **W**hy are math teachers good at solving detective stories?

They're quick at adding up clues.

704 **W**hat is the easiest way to get a day off school?

Wait until Saturday.

705 What is the robot's favorite part of school?

Assembly.

706 How many letters are in the alphabet?

Eleven. Count them -t-h-e-a-l-p-h-a-b-e-t!

707 Why can you believe everything a bearded teacher tells you?

They can't tell bald-faced lies.

708 Did you hear about the two history teachers who were dating?

They go to restaurants to talk about old times.

709 **D**id you hear about the teacher who wore sunglasses to give out exam results?

He took a dim view of his students' performance.

710 **H**ow does a math teacher know how long she sleeps?

She takes a ruler to bed.

711 **W**hat type of instruments did the early Britons play?

The Anglo-saxophone.

712 **W**hat do you call an art teacher who is always complaining?

Mona Lisa.

713 **T**eacher: *"Why are you eating candy in my classroom?"*
Ed: *"Because the shop had run out of gum."*

714 **W**hat word is always spelled wrong?

Wrong.

715 **M**ath teacher: *"Anne, why have you brought a picture of the queen of England with you today?"*

Anne: *"You told us to bring a ruler with us."*

716 **M**ath teacher: *"Richard, if you had 50 cents in each pants pocket, and $2 in each jacket pocket, what would you have?"*

Richard: *"Someone else's clothes, Sir."*

717 **W**hat kind of tests do witch teachers give?

Hex-aminations.

718 **S**tudent: *"I don't think I deserve a zero on this test."*

Teacher: *"Neither do I, but it was the lowest I could give you!"*

719 Teacher: *"Jessica, you aren't paying attention to me. Are you having trouble hearing?"*
Jessica: *"No, I'm having trouble listening."*

720 Teacher: *"You missed school yesterday, didn't you?"*
Student: *"Not very much."*

721 Student: *"I didn't do my homework because I lost my memory."*
Teacher: *"When did this start?"*
Student: *"When did what start?"*

722 Playing truant from school is like having a credit card.
Lots of fun now, pay later.

723 Teacher: *"Why didn't you answer me, Stuart?"*
Stuart: *"I did. I shook my head."*
Teacher: *"You don't expect me to hear it rattling from here, do you?"*

724 **W**hy was the principal worried?

Because there were so many rulers in the school.

725 **T**eacher: "I told you to stand at the end of the line."

Student: "I tried, but someone was already there."

726 **T**eacher: "I told you to draw a cow eating grass, but you've only drawn a cow."

Student: "The cow has eaten all the grass."

727 **T**eacher: "Why haven't you been to school for the past two weeks, Billy?"

Billy: "It's not my fault. Whenever I go to cross the road outside, there's a man with a sign saying 'Stop Children Crossing'!"

728 **D**id you hear about the teacher who locked the school band in a deep freeze?

They wanted to play really cool jazz.

729 **T**eacher: *"What bird doesn't build its own nest?"*

Student: *"The cuckoo."*

Teacher: *"That's right. How did you know that?"*

Student: *"Everyone knows cuckoos live in clocks!"*

730 **H**istory teacher: *"Why were ancient sailing ships so eco-friendly?"*

Student: *"Because they could go for hundreds of miles to the galleon."*

731 **M**ath teacher: *"If you multiplied 1,386 by 395, what would you get?"*

Student: *"The wrong answer."*

732 **W**hy did the boy throw his watch out of the window during a test?

Because he wanted to make time fly.

733 English teacher: *"James, give me a sentence with the word 'counterfeit' in it."*

James: *"I wasn't sure if she was a centipede or a millipede, so I had to count her feet."*

734 Computer teacher: *"Sarah, give me an example of software."*

Sarah: *"A floppy hat."*

735 *"What were you before you started school, girls and boys?"* asked the teacher, hoping that someone would say *"babies"*.

She was disappointed when all the children cried out, *"Happy!"*

736 Teacher: *"That's the stupidest boy in the whole school."*

Mother: *"That's my son."*

Teacher: *"Oh! I'm so sorry."*

Mother: *"You're sorry?"*

737 My teacher says I have such bad handwriting that I ought to be a doctor!

738 "I hope you're not one of those boys who sits and watches the school clock," said the principal to the new boy.

"No, Sir," he replied. "I have a digital watch that beeps at 3:15!"

A new watch, sonny?

It's 3:15 p.m. Tell the principal to go home.

739 Ben's teacher thinks Ben is a wonder child.

She wonders whether he'll ever learn anything.

740 "How old would you say I am, Francis?" the teacher asked.

"Forty," said the boy promptly.

"What makes you think I'm 40?" asked the puzzled teacher.

"My big brother is 20," he replied, "and you're twice as silly as he is!"

741 "I'm not going to school today," said Alexander to his mother. "The teachers bully me and the boys don't like me."

"That's not too surprising. You're 35 years old," replied his mother, "and you're the principal!"

742 "**W**hat do you like about your new school, Billy?" asked Uncle Ned.

"When it's closed!"

743 First teacher: "What's wrong with young Jimmy today? I saw him running around the playground, screaming and pulling at his hair."

Second teacher: "Don't worry. He's just lost his marbles."

744 **S**imple Simon was writing a geography essay for his teacher. It began like this:

The people who live in Paris are called parasites . . .

745 Teacher: *"Are you good at arithmetic?"*
Mary: *"Well, yes and no."*
Teacher: *"What do you mean, yes and no?"*
Mary: *"Yes, I'm no good at arithmetic."*

746 Home economics teacher: *"Joe, what are the best things to put in a chocolate cake?"*
Joe: *"Teeth!"*

747 Teacher: *"Your daughter's only 5 and she can spell her name backwards? Why, that's remarkable!"*
Mother: *"Yes, we're very proud of her."*
Teacher: *"And what is your daughter's name?"*
Mother: *"Anna."*

748 "What are three words most often used by students?" the teacher asked the class.
"I don't know," sighed a student.
"That's correct!" said the teacher.

749 Shane: *"Dad, today my teacher yelled at me for something I didn't do."*
Dad: *"What did he yell at you for?"*
Shane: *"For not doing my homework."*

750 Teacher: *"If you had one dollar and asked your dad for one dollar, how much money would you have?"*

Student: *"One dollar."*

Teacher: *"Are you sure?"*

Student: *"Yes, my dad wouldn't give me a dollar."*

751 Teacher: *"Billy, stop making ugly faces at the other students!"*

Billy: *"Why?"*

Teacher: *"When I was your age, I was told that if I kept making ugly faces, my face would stay that way."*

Billy: *"Well, I can see you didn't listen."*

Silly Book Titles

752 *My Golden Wedding* by Annie Versary

753 *The Terrible Problem* by Major Setback

754 *A Load of Old Rubbish* by Stephan Nonsense

755 *Tape Recording for Beginners* by Cass Ette

756 *Don't Leave Without Me* by Isa Coming

757 *When Shall We Meet Again?* by Miles Apart

758 *The Atlantic Ocean* by I. C. Waters

759 *Return of the Prodigal* by Gretta Sonne

760 *Will He Win?* by Betty Wont

761 *Hair Disorders* by Dan Druff

762 *A Call For Assistance* by Linda Hand

763 *Pain and Sorrow* by Anne Guish

764 *Garden Water Features* by Lily Pond

765 *Crossing Roads Safely* by Luke Bothways

766 *Sunday Service* by Neil Downe

767 *The Laser Weapon* by Ray Gunn

768 *Lost in the Desert* by Diana Thirst

769 *Truthful Tales* by Frank Lee

770 *Romantic Remembrance* by Valentine Card

771 *Making the Most of Life* by Maxie Mumm

772 *Making the Least of Life* by Minnie Mumm

773 *The Japanese Way of Death* by Harri Kirri

774 *Repairing Old Clothes* by Fred Bare

775 *Winter Heating* by Ray D. Ater

776 *Don't Wake the Baby* by Elsie Cries

777 *Out for the Count* by Esau Stars

778 *The Strongman* by Everhard Muscles

779 *The Best Day Ever* by Trudy Light

780 *The Sad Woman* by Paul Aidy

781 *Making Millions* by Ivor Lott

782 *Pig Breeding* by Lena Bacon

783 *Kidnapped!* by Caesar Quick

A poor millionaire

784 *The Haunted Room* by Hugo First

785 *Making Weatherproof Clothes* by Ranier Day

786 *Late Again* by Misty Buss

787 *Beginning Magic* by Beatrix Star

788 *Making Snacks* by San Widge

789 *Grand Canyon Adventures* by Rhoda Donkey

790 *Winning* by Vic Tree

791 *The Big Bang* by Dinah Mite

792 *The Garlic Eater* by I. Malone

793 *Modern Haircuts* by Sean Head

794 *Shipwrecked!* by Mandy Lifeboats

795 *Dangerous Germs* by Mike Robes

796 *Igloo Building* by S. Keemo

797 *Smashing Glass* by Eva Stone

Every igloo starts with the first block of ice

Please empty me. LITTER

798 *The Hurricane* by Rufus Blownoff

799 *Carpet Fitting* by Walter Wall

800 *Litter Collection* by Phil D. Basket

801 *Summer Bites* by Amos Quito

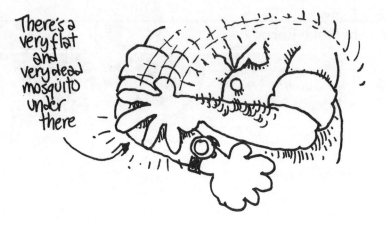

802 *Vegetable Gardening* by Rosa Cabbages

803 *Improve Your Garden* by Anita Lawn

804 *Quick Breakfasts* by Roland Butter

805 *Weekend Breaks* by Gladys Friday

806 *Keep on Trying* by Percy Vere

807 *Cheese and Lunchmeat Dishes* by Della Katessen

808 *Country Dancing* by Hans Kneesanboomsadaisy

809 *Catching Criminals* by Hans Upp

810 *The Runaway Horse* by Gay Topen

811 *A Bang on the Head* by Esau Stars

812 *How to Make Money* by Robin Banks

813 *Hide and Seek* by I. C. Hugh

814 *Seasons Greetings* by Mary Christmas

815 *The Wrong Shoe* by Titus Canbe

A GHOST OF A WITCH

816 *The Ghost of a Witch* by Eve L. Spirit

817 *How to Feed Werewolves* by Nora Bone

818 *Reaching the Top* by Ella Vator

819 *The Broken Vase* by Alex Plain

820 *Always Late* by Chester Minnit

821 *Collecting Reptiles* by Croc A. Dile

822 *Swallowing Dr Jekyll's Potion* by Iris Keverything

823 *A Ghost in My House* by Olive N. Fear

824 *Adding Up* by Juan and Juan

825 *The Chocolate Bar* by Ken I. Havesum

826 *The Lady Artist* by Andrew Pictures

827 *The Leaky Tap* by Constant Dripping

828 *In the Summer* by Clement Weather

829 *Telephone Problems* by Ron Number

830 *Aching Joints* by Arthur Itis

831 *Bird Watching* by Mac Caw

832 *The TV Guide* by Watson Telly

PARTY PARTY PARTY

833 *Buying Insurance* by Justin Case

834 *Whodunit?* by Iva Clew

835 *Hosting a Party* by Maude D. Merrier

836 *Winning the Lottery* by Jack Potts

837 *Robbers Who Got Away With It* by Hugh Dunnit

838 *Classic Furniture* by Ann Teaks

839 *Keeping Pet Snakes* by Sir Pent

840 *The Omen* by B. Warned

841 *Mean Cats* by Claude Bottom

842 *The Bad Tempered Werewolf* by Claudia Armoff

843 *The Vampire's Victim* by E. Drew Blood

844 *Never Make a Witch Angry* by Sheila Tack

845 *Ghost Stories* by I.M. Scared

846 *Hunting Vampires* by Count Miout

847 *Witch in the Mirror* by Douglas Cracked

848 *The Funniest Monster* by Buster Gutt

849 *Hanging From a Cliff* by Alf Hall

850 *The Hungry Bear* by Aida Lott

851 *There's a Wizard at my Door* by Wade Aminit

852 *Monsters I Have Known* by O. Penjaw

853 *Christmas Traditions* by Miss L. Toe

854 *Creature from Another World* by A. Lee-En

855 *I Saw a Ghost* by Denise R. Knockin

856 *In the Cannibal's Cauldron* by Mandy Ceased

857 *Boo!* by Terry Fied

858 *I Met a Vampire* by Pearce Nex

859 *Collecting Mosquitoes* by Lara Bites

860 *How to Keep Out a Vampire* by Dora Steele

861 *Brides and Grooms* by Marie Mee

862 *Getting Your Homework Done* by Mae B. Tomorrow

863 *The Hungry Giant* by Ethan D. Lot

864 *Escape from the Monster* by Jess N. Time

865 *Catching Crooks* by Laura Norder

866 *Making Enemies From Your Friends* by Olive Alone

867 *My Crystal Ball* by C. A. Lot

Space

868 **W**hy did the boy become an astronaut?

Because he had his head in the stars.

869 **W**hat creates the most housework in alien homes?

Stardust.

870 **W**here do astronauts leave their space ships?

At parking meteors!

871 **W**hat do you call the bugs on the moon?

Luna-tics

872 **H**ow do you get a baby astronaut to sleep?

You rock-et!

873 What's an astronaut's favorite game?

Moonopoly!

874 How do spacemen pass the time on long trips?

They play astronauts and crosses!

875 Why does meat taste better in space?

Because it's meteor!

876 Why did Captain Kirk go into the ladies' toilet?

To boldly go where no man has gone before!

877 First astronaut: *"I'm hungry."*

Second astronaut: *"So am I. It must be launch time."*

878 Can I have a return ticket to the moon please?

Sorry the moon's full tonight.

879 **W**hat do you call a space magician?

A flying sorcerer!

880 **"I** want to be an astronaut when I grow up."

"What high hopes you have!"

881 **W**hat do you call an overweight E.T.?

An extra cholesterol.

882 **W**hat did the metric alien say?

"Take me to your liter!"

883 **W**hat did the alien say to the gas pump?

"Don't you know it's rude to stick your finger in your ear?"

884 **H**ow does a robot alien shave?

With a laser blade!

885 **W**hat do you call a robot who takes the longest route?

R2 Detour!

886 **W**hat holds the moon up?

Moonbeams!

Sport

887 **W**hat job does Dracula have with the Transylvanian baseball team?

He's the bat boy.

888 **W**hy is bowling the quietest sport?

Because you can hear a pin drop.

889 **"I** can't see us ever finishing this bowling game."

"Why is that?"

"Every time I knock all the pins down, someone calls a strike!"

Now when you get out there... I want to see HOME RUNS from you guys!

890 **W**hat part of a football field smells the best?

The scenter spot!

891 **W**hy aren't football stadiums built in outer-space?

Because there is no atmosphere!

892 **W**hich goalkeeper can jump higher than a crossbar?

All of them. A crossbar can't jump!

893 **W**hy did the soccer star hold his shoe to his ear?

Because he liked sole music!

894 **W**hat are Brazilian soccer fans called?

Brazil nuts!

895 **W**here do football players dance?

At a foot ball!

896 **W**hat sort of
nails do you find
in football shoes?

Toenails.

897 **W**hat lights up a
football stadium?

*A good football
game!*

898 **H**ow do you start a doll's race?

Ready, Teddy, Go!

899 **W**hy wouldn't the
coach let elephants
on the swim team?

*He was afraid they
would drop their
trunks.*

900 **H**ow do hens
encourage their
favorite basketball
teams?

They egg them on!

901 **W**ho won the race
between two balls
of string?

They were tied!

902 **H**ow did the basketball court get wet?

The players dribbled all over it!

903 **W**hy don't grasshoppers go to baseball games?

They prefer a game of cricket.

904 **W**hy didn't the dog want to play football?

It was a boxer!

905 **W**hy does a polo player ride a horse?

Because they're too heavy to carry.

906 **H**ow do you stop squirrels from playing football in the yard?

Hide the ball, it drives them nuts!

907 **W**hy should you be careful when playing against a team of big cats?

They might be cheetahs!

908 **W**hy do football coaches bring suitcases along to away games?

So that they can pack the defense!

909 **N**ame a tennis player's favorite city.

Volley Wood

910 **W**hy was the team manager shaking the cat?

To see if there was any money in the kitty!

911 **W**here do football coaches go when they are sick of the game?

The bored room!

912 Coach: *"I thought I told you to lose weight. What happened to your three week diet?"*

Player: *"I finished it in three days!"*

913 Coach: *"Our new player cost $10 million. I call him our wonder player."*

Fan: *"Why's that?"*

Coach: *"Every time he plays, I wonder why I bothered to draft him!"*

914 Coach: *"I'll give you $100 a week to start, and $500 a week in a year."*

Baseball player: *"See you in a year!"*

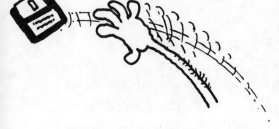

915 What happens when an athlete gets angry with his computer?

He becomes a floppy diskus thrower.

916 **W**hy aren't turkeys allowed to play football?

Because they always use fowl language.

917 **W**here do old bowling balls end up?

In the gutter!

918 **W**hy do artists never win when they play basketball?

They keep drawing the foul!

919 **W**hat did they call Dracula when he refereed the World Series?

The Vumpire!

920 **W**hy does someone who runs marathons make a good student?

Because education pays off in the long run!

921 **W**hat is a runner's favorite subject in school?
Jog-raphy!

922 **W**hat stories do basketball players tell?
Tall tales!

Crazy Fools

923 **D**id you hear
about the fool
who hijacked a
submarine?

*He demanded
$2 dollars and a
parachute.*

924 **W**hy did the
crazy sailor
grab some
soap when his
ship sank?

*Because he
thought he
would wash
ashore.*

925 **D**id you hear about the crazy sailor who was
discharged from his submarine duties?

He was found sleeping with the window open.

926 **A** crazy bank robber rushes into a bank, points two fingers at the teller and says,

"This is a muckup."

"Don't you mean a stickup?" said the teller.

"No. It's a muckup," replied the robber. *"I've forgotten my gun!"*

927 **"S**o you took your medicine right after your bath?" the doctor asked his crazy patient.

"No, doctor," replied the fool.

"By the time I'd drunk the bath, I had no room left for the medicine!"

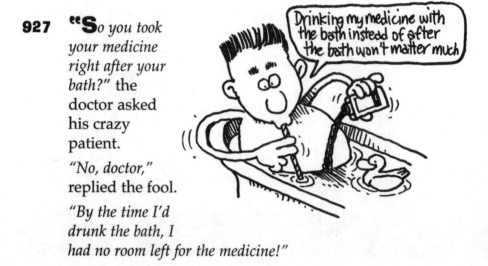

928 **D**id you hear about the crazy cyclist who won the Tour de France?

He did a lap of honor.

929 **W**hy did the team of fools always lose the tug-of-war?

They pushed.

930 Did you hear about the foolish karate champion who joined the army?

The first time he saluted, he nearly killed himself.

ATTENN-SHUNNN!

WAK-

931 The teacher told the crazy fool she knew he'd skipped school last Friday, and heard he'd been playing games at the arcade.

The fool told her it wasn't true – and he had the baseball game tickets to prove it!

B-LUR-BLH
(ROVER)

932 How does a fool call his dog?

He puts two fingers in his mouth and shouts "Rover!"

933 The fool saw a sign outside a police station that read *Man Wanted For Robbery,* and went in and applied for the job!

934 **D**id you hear about the crazy photographer?

He saved used light bulbs for his dark room.

935 **H**ave you heard about the fool who thinks a fjord is a Scandinavian motor car?

936 **W**hen the fool's co-worker asked why he had a sausage stuck behind his ear, he replied, "Oh... I *must have eaten my pencil for lunch!*"

937 **T**he gang's boss was surprised to find one of his gang sawing the legs off his bed.

"Why are you doing that?" he asked.

"Well, you did ask me to lie low for a bit," the fool replied.

938 **"Y**our finger is in *my soup bowl!"* said the man.

"Don't worry," said the foolish waiter. *"The soup isn't hot."*

939 **S**usie asked the fool if his tent leaked when he was on vacation.

"Only when it rained," he said.

940 **W**hy did the crazy pilot land his plane on a house?

Because the homeowner had left the landing lights on.

941 **"A**re you lost?" the policeman asked the foolish schoolgirl.

"Of course not," she replied. *"I'm here, it's my school that's lost."*

942 **D**id you hear about the crazy hitchhiker?

He got up early so there wouldn't be much traffic around.

943 **H**ave you heard about the fool who went into a store open 24 hours and asked what time they closed?

What do you call

944 ...a fairy who never takes a bath?

Stinkerbell!

945 ...a man with a paper bag on his head?

Russell!

MY LUNCH SHOULD BE IN HERE SOMEWHERE!

RUSTLE

RUSTLE

RUSTLE

946 ...a man with a seagull on his head?

Cliff!

947 ...a man who had an accident?

Derek!

948 ...a man with a map on his head?

Miles!

949 . . . a flying policeman?

Heli-copper!

950 . . . a carrot who talked back to the cook?

A fresh vegetable!

951 . . . a skunk in a courthouse?

Odor in the court!

952 . . . the chief's daughter when she's in trouble?

Miss Chief!

953 . . . a man with a large black and blue mark on his head?

Bruce!

954 . . . a man with some cat scratches on his head?

Claude!

955 . . . an egg laid by a dog?

A pooched egg!

956 . . . a boy with an encyclopedia in his pants?
Smarty pants.

957 . . . a train full of gum?
A chew chew train!

The new season's windswept look

958 . . . a woman standing in a breeze?
Gail!

959 . . . a woman with a tortoise on her head?
Shelley!

MEOW...

FIRST AID KIT

960 . . . a cat that joined the Red Cross?
A first aid kit!

961 . . . a rabbit locked in a sauna?
A hot cross bunny!

962 . . . a man with a legal document?
Will!

963 . . . a man with a truck on his head?
Deceased!

Wicked

964 **"D**addy, can I have another glass of water, please?"

"Okay, but that's the twelfth one I've given you tonight."

"Yes I know, but my bedroom is still on fire."

965 **W**hat's the difference between school lunches and a pile of slugs?

School lunches are on plates.

966 **J**ohn: *"Do you know anyone who has gone on the television?"*

Wendy: *"Just my dog, but he's housetrained now."*

967 **D**id you hear about the two fat men who ran a marathon?

One ran in short bursts, the other ran in burst shorts.

968 **W**hy are naughty kids like maggots?

Because they try to wriggle out of everything.

969 **A** woman woke her husband in the middle of the night.

"There's a burglar in the kitchen eating the cake I made!" she said.

"Who should I call?" asked her husband. "The police or an ambulance?"

970 **M**y cousin spent a bundle on deodorant, until he found out people just didn't like him . . .

971 **D**id you hear about the two bodies cremated at the same time?

It was a dead heat.

972 **D**id you hear about the dentist who became a brain surgeon?

His drill slipped.

973 **W**hat did they prove when the steam roller ran over the fat man?

That he had lots of guts.

974 **B**oy: *"Dad there's a black cat in the dining room!"*

Dad: *"That's okay son, black cats are lucky."*

Son: *"This one is— he's eating your dinner!"*

975 **T**he cruise ship passenger was feeling really seasick, when the waiter asked if he'd like some lunch.

"No thanks," he replied.

"Just throw it over the side and save me the trouble."

976 **A** mushroom walks onto the playground and asks *"Can I play?"*

But the other kids refuse.

The mushroom says, *"Why not? I'm a fun-gi!"*

977 **H**airdresser: "Would you like a haircut?"

Boy: "No, I'd like them all cut."

978 **S**he's so ugly that when a wasp stings her, it has to shut its eyes!

979 A man out for a walk came across a little boy pulling his cat's tail.

"Hey you!" he shouted. *"Don't pull the cat's tail!"*

"I'm not pulling," replied the boy. *"I'm only holding on. The cat's doing the pulling!"*

980 There's no point in telling some people a joke with a double meaning.

They wouldn't understand either of them!

981 George is the type of boy that his mother doesn't want him to hang around with . . .

982 Three guys, Shutup, Manners, and Poop, were walking down the road when Poop fell down. Shutup went to get help. He found a policeman who asked, *"What's your name?"*

"Shutup," he answered.

"Hey, where are your manners!" the policeman exclaimed.

Shutup replied, *"Outside on the road, picking up Poop!"*

983 Three girls walked into a beauty shop. Two had blonde hair and one had green hair. The stylist asked the blondes, *"How did you get to be blonde?"*

"Oh, it's natural," they replied.

The stylist asked the other girl, *"How did your hair become green?"*

She replied, *"Rub your hand on your nose and then across your hair."*

984 **F**ather: *"Johnny got an A on his assignment! I think he got his brains from me."*

Mother: *"I think you're right. I've still got mine."*

985 **S**am: *"Mom, can I have a pony for Christmas?"*

Mom: *"Of course not. You'll have turkey just like the rest of us."*

986 **A** fat man went into a cafe and ordered two slices of apple pie with four scoops of ice cream, covered with whipped cream and piled high with chopped nuts.

"Would you like a cherry on top?" asked the waitress.

"No thanks," said the man. *"I'm on a diet."*

987 Davey: *"Dad, there's a man at the door collecting for a new swimming pool."*

Dad: *"Alright, give him a glass of water."*

988 Have you ever seen a man-eating tiger?

No, but in a restaurant I once saw a man eating chicken.

989 What do you get when an elephant stands on your roof?

Mushed rooms.

990 A man came running out of his house as the garbage truck was driving by.

Man: *"Did I miss the garbage collection?"*

Garbage man: *"No, jump in."*

991 What did the dragon say when he saw the knight in his shining armor?

"Oh no! Not more canned food!"

992 What do you get when you cross a vampire with a dwarf?

A monster that sucks blood out of people's kneecaps.

993 The mother monster asked her son what he was doing with a saw, and if he'd seen his brother.

"You mean my new half-brother?" he replied!

994 Where would you get a job playing an elastic trumpet?

In a rubber band!

995 What is a volcano?

A mountain with the hiccups.

996 **W**hat goes in many different colors but always comes out blue?

A swimmer on a cold day!

997 **W**hy does the ocean roar?

Because there are oysters in its bed!

998 **W**hat do you call a one-legged woman?

Eileen!

Officer... I didn't even see it coming! It was a complete ax-ident!

999 **W**hose fault is it when an ax hits a car?

No one's, it's an ax-ident.

1000 One Sunday morning, a little old lady saw a boy walking through the park carrying a fishing pole and a jar of tadpoles.

"*Young man,*" she said. "*You shouldn't be going fishing on a Sunday?*"

"*I'm not going fishing, Ma'am,*" he called back. "*I'm going home!*"

1001 A man was on a full subway, when a heavy woman next to him said, "*If you were a gentleman, you'd stand up and let someone else sit down.*"

The man replied, "*And if you were a lady, you'd stand up and let four people sit down.*"

Recettes
vite vite vite !

Héloïse Martel

FIRST
Editions

Recettes vite vite vite !

© Éditions First-Gründ, Paris, 2010
60, rue Mazarine
75006 Paris – France
Tél. 01 45 49 60 00
Fax 01 45 49 60 01
Courriel : firstinfo@efirst.com
Internet : www.editionsfirst.fr

ISBN : 978-2-7540-1872-2
Dépôt légal : 2e trimestre 2010
Imprimé en Italie
Chez Legoprint
11 Via Galiléo Galiléi - 38 015 Lavis

Mise en page : KN Conception
Couverture : Olivier Frenot

Introduction

« Si j'avais du temps, j'adorerais préparer des petits plats. » Combien de fois avez-vous regretté que votre rythme de vie vous prive du plaisir de cuisiner ! Vous êtes las des surgelés réchauffés, des plats commandés, des sous-vides et des barquettes de salades toutes prêtes. Vous voulez éviter toutes les mauvaises graisses et les colorants suspects, surveiller votre budget, manger bon et bien. Incompatible avec le boulot, métro, dodo ? Pas vraiment, si vous choisissez des recettes rapides, simples et pourtant savoureuses, esthétiques et originales.

Organisez votre cuisine

Chaque seconde compte, chaque pas aussi. Économisez votre temps et votre énergie en organisant astucieusement votre cuisine.
- ayez les ustensiles courants à portée de main : couteaux, épluche-légumes, verre doseur, plats, poêles, casseroles.

- Rangez les ingrédients usuels au même endroit, dans les placards, dans le frigo ou le congélo. Rien de plus agaçant que de vider tout le frigo pour retrouver le bouquet de persil et le trouver collé contre la paroi givrée…
- Planifiez vos menus de la semaine à l'avance, vous pourrez ainsi faire toutes vos courses en une fois, et éviter les achats en rentrant du bureau.
- Ayez dans vos placards des ingrédients pour improviser en 3 minutes une salade sympa : herbes séchées, bocaux d'aromates, huiles et vinaigres aromatisés…
- Mettez les ustensiles de cuisine dans l'évier au fur et à mesure de leur utilisation, faites-les tremper, le nettoyage sera plus facile après le repas.
- Privilégiez les cocottes qui passent à table pour éviter les plats de service.

Faites des achats « gain de temps »

Certains produits du commerce sont vraiment hyper pratiques et font gagner un temps précieux.

- Achetez des légumes surgelés épluchés et émincés ; tout compte fait, ils ne sont pas beaucoup plus chers que les légumes frais. C'est particulièrement utile pour les oignons, les échalotes, l'ail, mais aussi pour les carottes et les poireaux en rondelles, les haricots verts, les épinards, les brocolis.

- Ayez en stock des coulis de fruits et des glaces pour réaliser en 3 minutes un dessert classique mais toujours apprécié, ainsi que des fruits secs (noix, noisettes, amandes, pistaches).
- Idem pour les sauces, pistou et autre bolognaise avec lesquelles vous préparez en 10 minutes un très bon plat de pâtes.
- Idem aussi pour les pâtes feuilletées, brisées ou sablées, pour réaliser des tartes cuites en 20 ou 30 minutes, pendant que vous mettez le couvert ou dégustez l'entrée.

Organisez-vous bien

Lisez les recettes à l'avance pour vous assurer que vous disposez bien de tous les ingrédients. Sortez-les sur le plan de travail. Prenez soin d'enchaîner les différentes étapes d'une recette de façon à gagner du temps. Si vous recevez, essayez de prévoir un menu qui ne vous oblige pas à tout préparer au dernier moment. Une bonne solution : une entrée prête la veille, ou un plat principal à réchauffer doucement.

Pour diminuer les temps de cuisson, émincez, hachez, divisez en portions et utilisez quatre ramequins plutôt qu'un grand moule pour vos gâteaux, crumbles…

Si un soir vous disposez d'un peu de temps, préparez les plats pour les jours où vous prévoyez de rentrer tard (gym, piscine, ou réunion qui risque de se prolonger…).

Les 150 recettes proposées dans ce petit livre sont prévues pour être préparées en un temps maximal de 10 minutes, la cuisson pouvant prendre 20 minutes au maximum. Certaines recettes, prêtes en 10 minutes sont signalées par ⏱, pour vous aider à foncer les jours de grosse pression.

Chacun trouvera ses recettes fétiches :
Pour les amateurs d'exotisme, le duo guacamole et surimi, le bœuf aux oignons et au gingembre et les litchis à la rose.
Pour les solides appétits, la mousse de sardines, la salade alsacienne et les petits gâteaux moelleux aux noisettes.

Pour les accrocs du light, le mesclun aux herbes et à l'orange, les crevettes sautées aux légumes et les yaourts à la fleur d'oranger.

Pour les gourmets raffinés, les œufs brouillés aux copeaux de parmesan, les rougets au bacon et les figues fraîches à la brousse, miel et cannelle.

Vite, vite, vite, la gourmandise n'attend pas !

ENTRÉES EXPRESS

•

BRICKS DE SARDINES

4 pers. **Préparation : 10 min** **Cuisson : 10 min**

4 feuilles de brick • 2 boîtes de sardines à l'huile • 4 pétales de tomate confite • 6 branches de coriandre • 40 g de beurre • poivre

Réalisation

Préchauffez le four à 240 °C (th. 8). Coupez les pétales de tomate en petits dés, ciselez la coriandre. Égouttez les sardines, écrasez-les à la fourchette dans un bol, ajoutez les dés de tomate et la coriandre, poivrez. Faite fondre le beurre dans une casserole.

Coupez les feuilles de brick en deux, superposez les deux moitiés sur le plan de travail. Placez au centre un peu de hachis de sardine, refermez en chausson. Badigeonnez les feuilles de brick de beurre, déposez-les dans un plat et faites dorer au four pendant 5 à 8 minutes en les retournant. Servez chaud ou tiède.

Notre conseil : accompagnez d'une petite salade de mesclun à l'huile d'olive.

BROCHETTES ITALIENNES

4 pers.   **Préparation : 15 min**

8 billes de mozzarella • 8 tranches très fines de jambon de Parme • 8 tomates cerise • 1 gousse d'ail • 4 tranches de pain de campagne • 3 cuil. à soupe d'huile d'olive • 8 feuilles de basilic

Réalisation

Pelez l'ail. Faites griller les tranches de pain, frottez-les d'ail, badigeonnez-les d'huile, coupez-les en cubes. Enfilez sur huit brochettes une tomate cerise, une feuille de basilic, une bille de mozzarella, une tranche de jambon roulée sur elle-même, deux cubes de pain. Servez à l'apéritif ou en entrée sur des petites assiettes.

BRUSCHETTAS AU JAMBON ET AU PARMESAN

4 pers. **Préparation : 10 min** **Cuisson : 5 min**

4 tranches de pain de campagne • 2 tranches de jambon d'Aoste • 2 tomates • 4 cuil. à soupe de parmesan râpé • 1 gousse d'ail • 2 cuil. à soupe d'huile d'olive • sel, poivre

Réalisation

Épluchez la gousse d'ail, frottez-en les tranches de pain, puis badigeonnez-les d'huile.

Pelez et épépinez les tomates, coupez la chair en tranches fines, déposez-les sur le pain. Coupez les tranches de jambon en deux, posez chaque moitié sur les tomates. Saupoudrez de parmesan, salez, poivrez, arrosez avec le reste d'huile.

Mettez les tranches de pain dans un plat à gratin et passez sous le gril du four pendant environ 5 minutes, pour que le fromage fonde et dore. Dégustez sans attendre.

CABÉCOUS PANÉS AU SÉSAME ⏰

4 pers. **Préparation : 5 min** **Cuisson : 5 min**

> 4 cabécous • 1 œuf • 6 cuil. à soupe de graines de sésame
> • 2 cuil. à soupe d'huile d'olive • sel, poivre

Réalisation

Battez l'œuf dans une assiette creuse avec du sel et du poivre, versez les graines de sésame dans une seconde assiette. Faites chauffer l'huile dans une poêle à revêtement antiadhésif.

Trempez les cabécous successivement dans l'œuf battu et les graines de sésame, puis déposez-les dans la poêle. Faites frire sur une face, retournez les fromages dès que la première face est dorée et poursuivez la cuisson encore quelques minutes. Déposez les cabécous sur des assiettes. Servez chaud.

Notre conseil : accompagnez ces cabécous panés de salades vertes mélangées.

CAPPUCCINO DE CHÂTAIGNES AU BACON

4 pers. **Préparation : 10 min** **Cuisson : 5 min**

1 bocal de soupe de châtaignes • 6 tranches de bacon • 20 cl de crème fleurette • poivre du moulin

Réalisation

Placez la crème au réfrigérateur plusieurs heures à l'avance. Versez la soupe de châtaignes dans une casserole, réchauffez-la à feu doux. Pendant ce temps, coupez les tranches de bacon en morceaux, faites-les griller à sec dans une poêle à revêtement antiadhésif.

Fouettez la crème liquide en chantilly au batteur électrique. Versez la soupe dans quatre bols, déposez dessus une grosse cuillerée de chantilly et piquez quelques morceaux de bacon. Donnez un tour de moulin à poivre et servez.

CASSOLETTES D'ESCARGOTS AUX CHAMPIGNONS ⏱

4 pers.   **Préparation : 5 min**   **Cuisson : 5 min**

48 escargots au naturel • 150 g de champignons de Paris en boîte • ½ rouleau de beurre d'escargot • poivre

Réalisation

Rincez et égouttez les escargots et les champignons, mettez-les dans une casserole, ajoutez le beurre coupé en petits morceaux. Réchauffez à feu moyen.

Dès que le beurre frémit, répartissez dans quatre cassolettes, donnez un tour de moulin à poivre et servez.

CÉLERI RÉMOULADE ET POMME VERTE AU MAGRET FUMÉ

4 pers. **Préparation : 15 min**

½ boule de céleri • 1 pomme verte • 2 sachets de magret de canard fumé • 1 bol de mayonnaise • 2 cuil. à soupe de curry

Réalisation

Pelez le céleri, épluchez la pomme, râpez-les. Mettez-les dans un saladier, ajoutez la mayonnaise et le curry, mélangez bien et répartissez sur quatre assiettes. Dégraissez les tranches de canard, mettez-les sur les assiettes. Servez frais.

CHAMPIGNONS CRUS À LA CORIANDRE ⏱

4 pers.   **Préparation : 10 min**

500 g de champignons de Paris • ½ botte de coriandre • 2 yaourts nature • 1 citron • 1 cuil. à café de moutarde forte • 1 cuil. à soupe d'huile d'olive • sel, poivre du moulin

Réalisation

Lavez et essuyez les champignons après avoir retiré le bout terreux. Émincez-les, arrosez-les de jus de citron pour qu'ils ne noircissent pas, mettez-les dans un saladier. Mélangez dans un bol les yaourts avec la moutarde et l'huile, salez, poivrez, ajoutez la coriandre ciselée, versez sur les champignons, mélangez et servez sans attendre.

Notre conseil : si vous n'aimez pas la coriandre, remplacez-la par du persil plat ou de la ciboulette.

CHÈVRE FRAIS, ANCHOIS ET TOMATES CONFITES ⏱

4 pers. **Préparation : 10 min**

2 chèvres frais • 8 filets d'anchois à l'huile • 8 pétales de tomate confite • 2 cuil. à soupe d'huile d'olive • 2 branches de basilic • poivre du moulin

Réalisation

Coupez les fromages en lamelles fines, disposez-les en rosace sur quatre petites assiettes. Coupez les anchois et les tomates en petits dés, parsemez-en le chèvre, arrosez d'un peu d'huile, poivrez généreusement et garnissez de feuilles de basilic ciselées. Servez bien frais.

Notre conseil : vous pouvez remplacer le basilic par des herbes de Provence et ajouter des olives noires.

CONCOMBRE AU CUMIN ⏱

4 pers.   **Préparation : 5 min**

2 concombres • 4 yaourts nature • 2 cuil. à soupe de cumin
en poudre • sel, poivre

Réalisation

Lavez les concombres sans les éplucher, émincez-les
au robot en très fines rondelles, mettez-les dans un
saladier, ajoutez les yaourts, du sel, du poivre et le
cumin, mélangez et servez.

CRÈME D'AVOCAT AU PIMENT ⏱

4 pers.   **Préparation : 10 min**

4 gros avocats mûrs • 2 citrons verts • 50 cl de bouillon
de légumes • 1 cuil. à soupe de harissa • 4 cuil. à soupe
d'huile d'olive

Réalisation

Mélangez dans un bol l'huile d'olive et la harissa.
Pressez les citrons verts. Ouvrez les avocats, retirez
le noyau, prélevez la chair. Mixez-la avec le jus des
citrons et le bouillon de légumes.

Versez la crème d'avocat dans quatre bols. Placez au frais jusqu'au moment de servir. Déposez une cuillerée à soupe d'huile d'olive épicée au centre des bols.

CRÈME DE THON, CÂPRES ET CIBOULETTE ⏱

4 pers. **Préparation : 5 min**

400 g de thon à l'huile • 2 cuil. à soupe de câpres • 12 brins de ciboulette • poivre du moulin

Réalisation

Ciselez la ciboulette. Mixez le thon avec son huile et les câpres, mélangez à la ciboulette, répartissez dans quatre verres. Donnez un tour de moulin à poivre puis servez bien frais.

CROUSTILLANTS DE CREVETTES À LA CORIANDRE

4 pers.   **Préparation : 10 min   Cuisson : 10 min**

16 crevettes cuites décortiquées • 4 feuilles de brick • ½ cuil. à café de paprika • ½ cuil. à café de cumin • 1 citron • 1 botte de coriandre • sel, poivre

Réalisation

Préchauffez le four à 210 °C (th. 7). Recouvrez la plaque du four de papier sulfurisé. Pressez le citron, hachez la coriandre. Mélangez dans un bol le jus de citron, la coriandre, le paprika, le cumin, du sel et du poivre.

Étalez les feuilles de brick sur un torchon humide, coupez-les en quatre. Dans chaque quartier de feuille, déposez une crevette et un peu de sauce au citron, refermez le brick en papillote, déposez-les au fur et à mesure sur le plat. Enfournez et laissez cuire pendant 10 minutes. Servez chaud.

Notre conseil : accompagnez de sauce piquante et servez sur un lit de salade verte.

ENDIVES ET POMMES AU SAUMON ⏱

4 pers. **Préparation : 10 min**

4 endives • 2 pommes vertes • 400 g de dés de saumon fumé • 1 œuf dur • 1 cuil. à soupe de moutarde douce • 4 cuil. à soupe de jus de citron vert • 3 cuil. à soupe d'huile d'olive • 1 cuil. à soupe de baies roses • 4 branches d'aneth • sel, poivre

Réalisation

Mélangez dans un bol la moutarde, le jus de citron, l'huile d'olive, du sel et du poivre. Retirez les feuilles flétries des endives, coupez les autres en lamelles. Mettez-les dans un saladier, ajoutez les dés de saumon. Pelez les pommes, râpez-les, ajoutez-les. Arrosez de sauce, mélangez. Hachez grossièrement l'œuf dur. Répartissez dans quatre coupes ou quatre verrines, parsemez d'œuf dur, de baies roses et d'aneth ciselé. Servez frais.

FAISSELLE AUX OIGNONS ET AUX ÉPICES ⏱

4 pers. **Préparation : 10 min**

400 g de faisselle • 1 gros oignon rouge • 2 cuil. à café de cumin • ½ cuil. à café de piment • sel

Réalisation
Pelez et hachez l'oignon. Versez la faisselle dans un saladier, ajoutez les épices, du sel et l'oignon haché. Vérifiez l'assaisonnement, répartissez dans quatre verrines. Servez très frais.

Notre conseil : vous pouvez ajouter un peu de concombre râpé et de la ciboulette.

FAISSELLES, FENOUIL ET POIVRE ⏱

4 pers. **Préparation : 5 min**

400 g de faisselle • 4 cuil. à soupe de graines de fenouil • 4 cuil. à soupe d'huile d'olive • fleur de sel, poivre du moulin

Réalisation
Fouettez la faisselle avec l'huile et les graines de fenouil. Répartissez-les dans quatre verres et

saupoudrez d'un peu de fleur de sel et de poivre du moulin. Servez bien frais.

FRISÉE, JAMBON, FROMAGE ET NOIX ⏱

4 pers. **Préparation : 10 min**

1 salade frisée • 200 g d'allumettes de jambon • 100 g de comté • 50 g de cerneaux de noix • 1 cuil. à soupe de moutarde • 2 cuil. à soupe de vinaigre de vin à la framboise • 4 cuil. à soupe d'huile de noix • sel, poivre

Réalisation

Rincez et essorez la frisée, mettez-la dans un saladier. Coupez le comté en petits dés, ajoutez-le ainsi que les allumettes de jambon et les cerneaux de noix. Battez la moutarde avec le vinaigre, du sel, du poivre et l'huile. Versez sur la salade et mélangez.

GASPACHO DE ROQUETTE

4 pers.   **Prép. : 10 min**   **Cuisson : 5 min**   **Réfrigération : 2 h**

400 g de roquette • 50 cl de bouillon de volaille • 20 cl de crème liquide • 2 cuil. à soupe d'huile d'olive • sel, poivre du moulin

Réalisation

Lavez et essorez la roquette. Faites chauffer l'huile dans une casserole, mettez la roquette, faites-la revenir pendant 3 minutes, puis arrosez de bouillon. Portez à ébullition, salez, retirez du feu et mixez avec 15 cl de crème. Laissez refroidir, puis placez au réfrigérateur.

Au moment de servir, répartissez dans quatre bols, versez quelques gouttes de crème au centre des bols et donnez un tour de moulin à poivre.

GUACAMOLE ET SURIMI ⏱

4 pers. **Préparation : 10 min**

4 gros avocats mûrs • 3 citrons • 1 piment oiseau • 4 petits oignons blancs • 4 bâtonnets de surimi • sel

Réalisation

Pressez les citrons, pelez les oignons. Pelez les avocats, prélevez la pulpe. Mixez-la avec le jus de citron, les oignons, le piment et un peu de sel.

Répartissez le guacamole dans quatre ramequins. Détaillez le surimi en petits dés, disposez-les dessus. Servez frais.

MESCLUN AUX HERBES ET À L'ORANGE ⏰

4 pers.   **Préparation : 10 min**

300 g de mesclun • 1 grosse orange • 4 branches de cerfeuil • 6 brins de ciboulette • 1 cuil. à soupe de vinaigre balsamique • 2 cuil. à soupe d'huile d'olive • 3 cuil. à soupe de jus d'orange • sel, poivre

Réalisation

Lavez et essorez le mesclun, répartissez-le sur quatre assiettes. Pelez l'orange, détachez les quartiers en retirant les peaux blanches, mettez-les sur les assiettes. Ciselez les herbes.

Mélangez dans un bol le vinaigre, l'huile et le jus d'orange avec du sel et du poivre, nappez-en la salade et parsemez d'herbes. Servez aussitôt.

MILLE-FEUILLES D'AVOCAT AU SAUMON CRU

4 pers. **Préparation : 15 min**

4 avocats mûrs • 400 g de saumon frais • 2 citrons • 6 cuil. à soupe de sauce de soja • 4 cuil. à soupe d'huile d'olive • 4 branches d'aneth • poivre

Réalisation

Pressez les citrons, versez le jus dans un bol, ajoutez la sauce de soja, l'huile et un peu de poivre. Coupez le saumon cru en lamelles. Réservez. Retirez l'écorce des avocats, ôtez le noyau et coupez la chair en lamelles.

Préparez les assiettes : disposez, en les intercalant, les lamelles de saumon et d'avocat, nappez-les de sauce. Ciselez l'aneth, parsemez-en les assiettes. Servez immédiatement.

Notre conseil : le poisson cru est un ingrédient qui exige des conditions d'hygiène très strictes ; utilisez un plan de travail parfaitement nettoyé et brossez-vous les mains et les ongles avec un puissant désinfectant avant de le manipuler.

MOUSSE DE PIQUILLOS ET CHÈVRE FRAIS ⏱

4 pers. **Préparation : 10 min**

12 piquillos • 1 chèvre frais • 1 gousse d'ail • 2 cuil. à soupe d'huile d'olive • 1 branche de basilic • sel, poivre

Pelez la gousse d'ail, effeuillez le basilic. Mixez-les avec le chèvre, les piquillos égouttés, l'huile, un peu de sel et de poivre. Répartissez dans quatre petits ramequins. Servez frais.

Notre conseil : accompagnez de pain de campagne grillé.

MOUSSE DE SARDINES ⏱

4 pers. **Préparation : 5 min**

24 sardines à l'huile • 4 petits oignons blancs • 1 cuil. à soupe de thym effeuillé • sel, poivre

Réalisation
Pelez les oignons. Retirez l'arête centrale et la peau des sardines. Mixez-les avec les oignons, le thym, un peu de sel et de poivre.

Répartissez dans quatre petits ramequins. Servez avec des tranches de pain de campagne grillées et un quart de citron.

PETITES TERRINES DE THON AU FROMAGE FRAIS ⏱

4 pers. **Préparation : 5 min**

400 g de thon au naturel • 1 fromage frais à l'ail et aux fines herbes • poivre du moulin

Réalisation

Égouttez le thon, mettez-le dans un saladier, ajoutez le fromage frais, mélangez à la fourchette avec un peu de poivre et répartissez dans quatre petites terrines. Servez frais avec du pain grillé.

PIZZETTAS CALZONE

4 pers.   **Préparation : 10 min**   **Cuisson : 15 min**

1 rouleau de pâte à pizza toute prête • 8 tranches de pancetta • 1 boule de mozzarella • 1 bocal de purée de tomates • 2 cuil. à soupe d'origan • 4 cuil. à soupe d'huile d'olive • sel, poivre

Réalisation

Préchauffez le four à 210 °C (th. 7). Recouvrez la plaque du four de papier sulfurisé. Coupez la mozzarella en lamelles. Partagez la pâte en quatre parties. Sur chacune, déposez un peu de purée de tomates, deux tranches de pancetta, des lamelles de mozzarella, saupoudrez d'origan, salez, poivrez et repliez chaque pizzetta en chausson, badigeonnez-les d'huile d'olive.

Déposez-les sur la plaque du four et faites cuire pendant 15 minutes. Servez chaud ou tiède.

RAVIOLES À LA CRÈME ET AUX HERBES ⏱

4 pers. **Préparation : 5 min** **Cuisson : 5 min**

1 paquet de ravioles • 20 cl de crème liquide • 1 bouquet de ciboulette • sel, poivre

Réalisation

Faites chauffer la crème dans une casserole, salez, poivrez. Réservez. Ciselez la ciboulette. Faites bouillir de l'eau salée dans une grande casserole, plongez-y les ravioles, et dès la reprise de l'ébullition, égouttez-les. Répartissez-les dans quatre coupelles, arrosez de crème et parsemez de ciboulette.
Servez aussitôt.

SALADE DE CHOU BLANC AUX RAISINS

4 pers.　**Préparation : 10 min**　**Cuisson : 3 min**

½ chou blanc • 30 g de raisins secs • 1 cuil. à soupe de sauce de soja • 1 cuil. à soupe de vinaigre de vin • 3 cuil. à soupe d'huile d'olive • 1 cuil. à café de moutarde forte • sel, poivre

Réalisation

Mettez les raisins secs dans un bol, couvrez-les d'eau chaude. Ciselez finement le chou, plongez-le dans une casserole d'eau bouillante salée pendant 3 minutes, égouttez-le.

Préparez la sauce en mélangeant la moutarde, le vinaigre, du sel et du poivre, la sauce de soja et l'huile. Mettez le chou dans un saladier, ajoutez les raisins égouttés et arrosez de sauce. Mélangez bien.

SALADE DE PARME AUX PISTACHES

4 pers. **Préparation : 15 min**

1 salade feuille de chêne • 4 figues fraîches • 8 tranches de jambon de Parme très fines • 1 cuil. à soupe de moutarde forte • 2 cuil. à soupe de vinaigre de xérès • 4 cuil. à soupe d'huile d'olive • 4 cuil. à soupe de pistaches concassées • sel, poivre

Réalisation

Lavez et essorez la salade. Coupez les figues en lamelles, le jambon en lanières. Préparez la sauce en fouettant la moutarde avec le vinaigre, l'huile, un peu de sel et de poivre.

Mettez la salade dans un saladier, déposez dessus les lamelles de figue, le jambon et arrosez de vinaigrette. Parsemez de pistaches. Servez aussitôt.

SALADE DE POIS CHICHES, TOMATES ET OLIVES

4 pers.   **Préparation : 15 min**

1 boîte de pois chiches • 4 tomates • 1 gros oignon rouge • 100 g d'olives noires • 4 cuil. à soupe d'huile d'olive • 12 brins de ciboulette • sel, poivre

Réalisation

Pelez et émincez l'oignon. Lavez et essuyez les tomates, coupez-les en lamelles fines. Rincez et égouttez les pois chiches.

Versez les ingrédients dans un saladier, arrosez d'huile, salez peu, poivrez, mélangez. Ajoutez les olives et parsemez de brins de ciboulette ciselés. Servez frais.

SALADE DE RAIE SAUCE GRIBICHE

4 pers. **Préparation : 10 min** **Cuisson : 10 min**

400 g d'ailes de raie surgelées • 1 salade feuille de chêne • 1 œuf dur • 2 cuil. à soupe de câpres • 2 branches de persil • 1 cuil. à soupe de moutarde forte • 2 cuil. à soupe de vinaigre de vin • 4 cuil. à soupe d'huile d'olive • sel, poivre

Réalisation

Faites bouillir de l'eau dans une grande casserole, plongez les ailes de raie dedans et laissez frémir pendant 10 minutes.

Pendant ce temps, lavez et essorez la salade, puis préparez la sauce : fouettez la moutarde avec le vinaigre, du sel et du poivre, puis versez l'huile en filet en continuant de mélanger. Hachez le persil, coupez l'œuf dur en petits dés, ajoutez à la sauce ainsi que les câpres.

Répartissez la salade sur quatre assiettes. Égouttez les ailes de raie, détachez la chair de l'arête et disposez le poisson sur les assiettes. Arrosez de sauce et servez.

Notre conseil : ajoutez des tomates cerise.

SALADE DE TOMATES, POIS CHICHES ET ROQUETTE AU CUMIN 🕐

4 pers.   **Préparation : 10 min**

1 boîte de pois chiches • 4 tomates • 1 oignon rouge • 1 poignée de roquette • 1 cuil. à soupe de cumin moulu • 4 cuil. à soupe d'huile d'olive • sel, poivre

Réalisation

Egouttez les pois chiches. Lavez et essuyez les tomates, coupez-les en dés. Pelez l'oignon, hachez-le grossièrement. Lavez et essorez la roquette.

Versez l'huile dans un saladier, ajoutez le cumin, du sel et du poivre. Ajoutez les pois chiches, les dés de tomate, l'oignon et la roquette. Mélangez au moment de servir.

SALADE POMME-CAROTTES AU CITRON ET AU MIEL ⏱

4 pers. **Préparation : 10 min**

400 g de carottes • 1 pomme verte • 1 citron • 2 cuil. à soupe de miel • 3 cuil. à soupe d'amandes effilées • sel, poivre

Réalisation

Pressez le citron. Mélangez le jus dans un bol avec un peu de sel, de poivre et le miel. Pelez les carottes et la pomme, râpez-les, mettez-les dans un saladier, arrosez-les de sauce et mélangez.

Répartissez dans quatre verrines. Faites griller les amandes effilées à sec dans une poêle à revêtement antiadhésif, parsemez-les sur la salade.

SAUMON FUMÉ, TARTARE POMME OIGNONS ⏱

4 pers.   **Préparation : 10 min**

4 tranches de saumon fumé en tranches • 1 pomme verte
• 4 petits oignons blancs • 30 cl de crème liquide • 1 cuil.
à soupe de raifort • ½ botte de ciboulette • sel, poivre

Réalisation

Fouettez la crème liquide avec le raifort, un peu de sel
et de poivre. Réservez. Ciselez finement la ciboulette.
Pelez les oignons et la pomme. Coupez l'un et l'autre
en petits dés, mélangez-les à la crème.
Étalez sur chaque assiette une tranche de saumon
fumé, et déposez dessus un peu de tartare pomme-
oignons. Servez très frais.

SAUMON FUMÉ, CHANTILLY AU RAIFORT

4 pers. **Préparation : 15 min**

4 tranches de saumon fumé • 4 petits oignons blancs • 20 cl de crème liquide • 1 cuil. à soupe de raifort • 4 branches d'aneth • 4 cuil. à café d'œufs de saumon

Réalisation

Placez la crème au réfrigérateur plusieurs heures à l'avance. Pelez les oignons, émincez-les. Ciselez l'aneth. Fouettez la crème liquide au batteur électrique en incorporant le raifort et l'aneth pour obtenir une crème chantilly mousseuse.

Disposez sur chaque assiette une tranche de saumon, quelques lamelles d'oignon et une grosse quenelle de chantilly. Décorez d'une cuillerée à café d'œufs de saumon.

SOUPE FROIDE DE COURGETTES À LA MENTHE

4 pers.   **Préparation : 10 min**   **Cuisson : 5 min**

4 courgettes • 2 yaourts nature brassés • 8 feuilles de menthe • 4 cuil. à soupe d'huile d'olive • 2 pincées de cumin en poudre • 2 pincées de piment d'Espelette • sel, poivre

Réalisation

Faites chauffer de l'eau dans une casserole. Lavez les courgettes puis détaillez-les en petits tronçons, mettez-les dans l'eau et laissez cuire pendant 5 minutes. Égouttez-les et rafraîchissez-les.

Mixez-les avec les yaourts, l'huile, du sel, du poivre et les épices. Répartissez dans quatre verres, décorez de feuilles de menthe ciselées.

SOUPE GLACÉE DE TOMATES AUX ÉPICES ⏲

4 pers. **Préparation : 10 min**

400 g de tomates pelées au naturel • 1 cuil. à café de sel de céleri • 1 cuil. à café de cumin en poudre • 1 yaourt nature velouté • 3 cuil. à soupe d'huile d'olive • 1 citron • 3 branches de persil plat • sel, poivre

Réalisation

Mixez les tomates avec leur jus, versez dans une soupière. Pressez le citron, versez le jus dans la soupière, ajoutez l'huile, le yaourt et les épices. Salez, poivrez.

Répartissez dans quatre verres, parsemez de persil finement ciselé. Servez glacé.

Notre conseil : pour que la soupe soit bien froide, placez la boîte de tomates à l'avance au réfrigérateur, ou ajoutez quelques glaçons.

SOUPE VERTE

4 pers. **Préparation : 10 min   Cuisson : 15 min**

1 botte d'asperges vertes • 1 concombre • 200 g de pousses
d'épinards • 2 oignons • 4 branches de menthe • 1 litre de
bouillon de légumes • poivre du moulin

Réalisation

Lavez et essuyez le concombre, émincez-le. Lavez et
épongez les pousses d'épinard. Pelez les asperges,
coupez-les en petits tronçons. Pelez et émincez
les oignons. Mettez les légumes dans une grande
casserole, couvrez de bouillon, portez à ébullition
et laissez cuire pendant 10 minutes.

Retirez les pointes d'asperge, réservez-les et mixez la
soupe. Versez dans quatre bols, décorez de pointes
d'asperge et donnez un tour de moulin à poivre.
Servez chaud ou froid.

TERRINES DE THON EXPRESS ⏱

4 pers. **Préparation : 10 min**

400 g de thon au naturel • 4 œufs durs • 6 pommes de terre cuites • 6 cornichons • 1 bol de mayonnaise • 100 g de fromage blanc • sel, poivre

Réalisation

Pelez les pommes de terre, coupez-les en petits dés. Détaillez les cornichons en dés également, hachez grossièrement les œufs durs, égouttez le thon. Mélangez-les dans un saladier.

Fouettez la mayonnaise avec le fromage blanc, salez, poivrez, ajoutez-les dans le saladier et mélangez. Répartissez la préparation dans quatre petites terrines individuelles, mettez au frais en attendant de servir.

Notre conseil : servez avec du pain de campagne grillé.

VELOUTÉ D'ASPERGES AU SAUMON

4 pers. **Préparation : 5 min   Cuisson : 5 min**

1 litre de velouté d'asperges en brique • 200 g de pavés de saumon • 4 cuil. à café de crème fraîche • 6 brins de cerfeuil

Réalisation

Faites chauffer le velouté dans une grande casserole. Coupez les pavés de saumon en dés, mettez-les dans le potage, prolongez la cuisson pendant 3 minutes. Répartissez dans quatre assiettes creuses, déposez au centre une cuillerée de crème et parsemez de cerfeuil ciselé. Servez bien chaud.

VELOUTÉ DE CAROTTES AU FENOUIL GRILLÉ ⏱

4 pers. **Préparation : 5 min   Cuisson : 3 min**

1 litre de jus de carotte • 4 cuil. à café de graines de fenouil • sel, poivre du moulin

Réalisation

Faites griller les graines de fenouil à sec dans une poêle à revêtement antiadhésif. Versez le jus de carotte dans quatre verres, salez, poivrez, décorez de fenouil grillé.

VELOUTÉ DE COURGETTES COCO CIBOULETTE

4 pers. **Préparation : 10 min** **Cuisson : 15 min**

4 grosses courgettes • 4 gousses d'ail • 2 cuil. à soupe d'huile d'olive • 30 g de noix de coco râpée • 6 brins de ciboulette • sel, poivre

Réalisation

Lavez et essuyez les courgettes, coupez-les en gros dés. Pelez l'ail. Faites chauffer l'huile dans une sauteuse, mettez l'ail et les courgettes, mélangez, salez, poivrez et arrosez avec 50 cl d'eau. Portez à ébullition, baissez le feu et laissez cuire pendant 10 minutes.

Mixez, versez dans des bols. Faites griller la noix de coco à sec dans une poêle, ciselez la ciboulette et saupoudrez-en les bols. Servez aussitôt.

Notre conseil : servez ce velouté froid en remplaçant la ciboulette par de la menthe. Vous pouvez aussi ajouter au velouté des dés de filet de poulet fumé ou des lardons grillés.

VERRINES DE SAUMON FUMÉ AU POIVRE VERT

4 pers.   **Préparation : 15 min**

400 g de saumon fumé • 1 cuil. à soupe de poivre vert en grains • 1 citron vert • 15 cl de crème liquide • sel, poivre

Réalisation

Placez la crème et les batteurs du fouet au réfrigérateur plusieurs heures à l'avance.

Pressez le citron vert. Mixez le saumon fumé avec les grains de poivre, le jus de citron, du sel et du poivre.

Fouettez la crème pour obtenir une chantilly ferme, mélangez à la crème de saumon, mettez dans des verrines. Servez bien frais.

Notre conseil : dégustez ces verrines avec des tranches de pain grillé.

VIANDE DES GRISONS, MELON, PISTACHES ⏱

4 pers. **Préparation : 5 min**

> 24 tranches de viande des Grisons • 1 melon • 1 citron vert
> • 4 cuil. à soupe d'huile d'olive • 4 cuil. à soupe de pistaches
> non salées, concassées • sel, poivre

Réalisation

Répartissez les tranches de viande sur quatre assiettes.
Pressez le citron vert, mélangez le jus avec l'huile
d'olive, du sel et du poivre, versez sur les tranches
de viande des Grisons.
Ouvrez le melon, retirez les graines et prélevez des
billes dans la chair avec une cuillère parisienne,
déposez-les sur la viande. Parsemez de pistaches
concassées. Servez aussitôt.

ŒUFS ULTRA-RAPIDES

•

BRICKS À L'ŒUF ET AU THON ⏲

4 pers. **Préparation : 5 min** **Cuisson : 5 min**

8 feuilles de brick • 4 œufs • 150 g de thon au naturel en boîte • 4 branches de coriandre • 3 cuil. à soupe d'huile d'olive • sel, poivre

Réalisation

Égouttez le thon, écrasez-le à la fourchette. Effeuillez et ciselez la coriandre.

Étalez sur un plan de travail les feuilles de brick deux par deux. Mettez au centre le thon et la coriandre. Cassez un œuf sur chaque feuille de brick et refermez-les en formant un portefeuille.

Faites chauffer l'huile dans une poêle, déposez délicatement les chaussons et faites-les frire à feu vif pendant 1 minute sur une face. Retournez-les, baissez le feu et faites-les frire sur l'autre face pendant 3 minutes environ. Le blanc d'œuf doit être pris et le jaune rester liquide.

Déposez les chaussons sur un papier absorbant, puis mettez-les sur les assiettes de service.

ŒUFS BROUILLÉS, COPEAUX DE PARMESAN ⊙

4 pers.   **Préparation : 5 min**   **Cuisson : 5 min**

10 œufs • 30 g de beurre • 1 cuil. à soupe de crème fraîche
• 30 g de parmesan • sel, poivre du moulin

Réalisation

Battez les œufs dans un saladier avec un peu de sel et
de poivre. Faites fondre le beurre dans une casserole,
versez les œufs et faites cuire à feu très doux sans
cesser de mélanger avec un fouet. Dès que les œufs
commencent à prendre, retirez la casserole du feu
et ajoutez la crème.

Répartissez sur quatre petites assiettes. Taillez des
copeaux dans le parmesan avec un épluche-légumes,
déposez délicatement sur les œufs. Donnez un tour
de moulin à poivre et servez.

ŒUFS COCOTTE, PISTOU, TOMATES CONFITES ET CROÛTONS

4 pers. Préparation : 15 min   Cuisson : 10 min

8 œufs extra frais • 4 cuil. à soupe de pistou (maison ou en bocal) • 4 pétales de tomate confites • 1/3 de baguette • 1 cuil. à soupe d'huile • sel, poivre

Réalisation

Préchauffez le four à 180 °C (th. 6). Préparez un bain-marie. Huilez légèrement quatre petites cocottes. Coupez la baguette en tranches fines, répartissez-les dans les cocottes. Cassez deux œufs par cocotte, versez un peu de pistou dessus et déposez 1 pétale de tomate confite. Enfournez et laissez cuire pendant 10 minutes.

ŒUFS COCOTTE, TOMATE ET CHORIZO

4 pers.   **Préparation : 10 min**   **Cuisson : 15 min**

> 4 œufs extra frais • 1 morceau de chorizo de 150 g • 4 tomates
> • 20 cl de crème fraîche • 2 cuil. à soupe d'huile d'olive
> • sel, poivre, sucre

Réalisation

Préchauffez le four à 240 °C (th. 8). Préparez un bain-marie. Huilez quatre petites cocottes. Coupez le chorizo en petits dés. Pelez et épépinez les tomates, coupez-les en cubes.

Faites chauffer le reste d'huile dans une sauteuse, faites dorer les dés de chorizo pendant 5 minutes, retirez-les. Mettez les tomates, salez, poivrez, ajoutez une bonne pincée de sucre, arrosez de crème et faites cuire pendant 3 minutes en mélangeant.

Répartissez la sauce aux tomates dans les cocottes, cassez un œuf dans chacune et déposez quelques dés de chorizo. Mettez les cocottes dans le bain-marie et faites cuire pendant 8 minutes. Servez aussitôt.

Notre conseil : vous pouvez varier cette recette avec des lardons fumés ou des allumettes de jambon. Accompagnez de mouillettes de pain grillé.

ŒUFS MAYONNAISE AU CUMIN

4 pers. **Préparation : 10 min** **Cuisson : 10 min**

6 œufs + 1 jaune • 200 g de pousses d'épinard • 1 cuil. à soupe de moutarde forte • 1 cuil. à café de cumin en poudre • 8 cuil. à soupe d'huile d'olive • ½ citron • sel, poivre

Réalisation

Faites durcir les six œufs dans une casserole d'eau bouillante pendant 10 minutes. Pendant ce temps, lavez et essorez les pousses d'épinard, répartissez-les sur quatre assiettes.

Préparez la mayonnaise : mélangez le jaune d'œuf avec la moutarde, un peu de sel et de poivre, versez l'huile en filet en fouettant. Incorporez le cumin et le jus du demi-citron.

Rafraîchissez les œufs, écalez-les. Ouvrez-les en deux dans le sens de la longueur. Déposez trois demi-œufs par assiette, nappez-les de mayonnaise. Servez frais.

ŒUFS MOLLETS, ÉPINARDS FRAIS

4 pers.   **Préparation : 10 min   Cuisson : 10 min**

8 œufs • 800 g d'épinards frais • 30 g de beurre • 10 cl de crème fraîche • sel, poivre du moulin

Réalisation

Lavez et essuyez les épinards, équeutez-les. Faites fondre le beurre dans une sauteuse, ajoutez les épinards, laissez-les cuire pendant 3 minutes en mélangeant, salez, poivrez et ajoutez la crème.

Portez à ébullition une grande casserole d'eau, mettez les œufs et comptez 7 minutes dès la reprise de l'ébullition. Retirez les œufs, rafraîchissez-les et écalez-les délicatement.

Répartissez les épinards à la crème dans quatre assiettes, déposez dessus deux œufs, donnez un tour de moulin à poivre et servez aussitôt.

ŒUFS MOLLETS ET MOUILLETTES D'ASPERGES

4 pers. **Préparation : 10 min** **Cuisson : 10 min**

8 œufs • 24 asperges vertes • 24 fines tranches de viande
des Grisons • 50 g de parmesan • 30 g de beurre • sel,
poivre du moulin

Réalisation

Pelez les asperges, retirez le bout fibreux. Enroulez
chaque asperge dans une tranche de viande des
Grisons. Faites fondre le beurre dans une poêle,
faites revenir les asperges pendant 5 minutes en les
retournant.

Faites cuire les œufs à l'eau bouillante pendant
7 minutes, rafraîchissez-les, écalez-les.

Placez sur chaque assiette deux œufs et six asperges.
Salez, poivrez et décorez de copeaux de parmesan.
Servez immédiatement.

OMELETTE CHÈVRE-ESTRAGON ⏰

4 pers.   **Préparation : 5 min**   **Cuisson : 5 min**

8 œufs • 1 chèvre frais • 1 branche d'estragon • 1 cuil.
à soupe d'huile d'olive • sel, poivre

Réalisation

Battez les œufs dans un saladier avec deux cuillerées
à soupe d'eau, salez, poivrez. Coupez le fromage en
petits dés et ciselez les feuilles d'estragon.

Faites chauffer l'huile dans une poêle, versez les œufs
et faites cuire l'omelette. Quand les œufs commencent
à prendre, ajoutez les dés de fromage et l'estragon.
Poursuivez la cuisson à feu très doux. Pliez l'omelette
en deux, faites-la glisser sur le plat de service. Servez
bien chaud.

OMELETTE HERBES ET FROMAGE

4 pers. **Préparation : 10 min** **Cuisson : 10 min**

8 œufs • 1 bouquet de persil plat • 1 bouquet de ciboulette
• 4 branches de basilic • 4 branches de menthe • 100 g de
gruyère râpé • 2 cuil. à soupe d'huile de tournesol • sel,
poivre, noix de muscade

Réalisation

Ciselez finement toutes les herbes, mettez-les dans un
saladier. Cassez les œufs, battez-les avec les herbes,
salez, poivrez, ajoutez un peu de noix de muscade
et le fromage râpé.

Faites chauffer l'huile dans une poêle, versez les œufs
et faites cuire l'omelette à feu moyen en soulevant les
bords. Lorsque les œufs sont pris, repliez l'omelette en
chausson et faites-la glisser sur un plat de service.

POISSONS ET CRUSTACÉS MINUTE

•

CABILLAUD À LA CHOUCROUTE

4 pers.   **Préparation : 5 min**   **Cuisson : 20 min**

4 pavés de cabillaud • 1 kg de choucroute cuite • 4 cl de vin blanc • 1 cuil. à soupe de baies de genièvre • 1 cuil. à soupe de graines de cumin • sel, poivre

Réalisation

Mettez le chou dans une cocotte, ajoutez les baies de genièvre et les graines de cumin, arrosez de vin blanc, couvrez et laissez réchauffer à feu doux pendant 10 minutes.

Faites cuire le cabillaud à la vapeur pendant 10 minutes.

Dressez la choucroute sur un plat, déposez dessus les pavés de cabillaud. Salez, poivrez et servez aussitôt.

CABILLAUD VAPEUR AU CURRY

4 pers.   **Préparation : 10 min   Cuisson : 8 min**

4 pavés de cabillaud • 1 cuil. à soupe de curry • 1 cuil.
à soupe d'huile d'olive • 1 cuil. à soupe de miel • 1 citron
non traité • sel, poivre

Réalisation

Faites bouillir de l'eau dans le compartiment inférieur
d'un cuit-vapeur. Râpez le zeste du citron, pressez le
fruit. Mélangez dans un bol le jus de citron, le miel,
l'huile d'olive, le curry, du sel et du poivre.
Déposez les pavés de poisson sur quatre feuilles de
papier sulfurisé, arrosez d'un peu de sauce, saupoudrez de zeste, fermez les papillotes et déposez-les
dans le panier supérieur du cuit-vapeur. Laissez cuire
pendant 6 à 8 minutes selon l'épaisseur des pavés.
Déposez les papillotes dans les assiettes et servez le
reste de sauce en saucière.

CREVETTES SAUTÉES AUX LÉGUMES

4 pers. **Préparation : 10 min** **Cuisson : 10 min**

600 g de crevettes roses • 250 g de cocos plats • 250 g de pois gourmands • 2 oignons • 4 branches de coriandre • 2 cuil. à soupe d'huile d'olive • 2 cuil. à soupe de graines de sésame • sel, poivre

Réalisation

Pelez et émincez les oignons, effilez les cocos et les pois gourmands.

Faites chauffer l'huile dans une sauteuse ou dans un wok, mettez les légumes, les crevettes, salez, poivrez, mélangez et laissez cuire à feu vif en mélangeant pendant 10 minutes. Faites griller à sec les graines de sésame. Répartissez les crevettes et les légumes dans quatre bols, parsemez de coriandre ciselée et de graines de sésame. Servez aussitôt.

GAMBAS À LA CORIANDRE

4 pers. **Préparation : 15 min** **Cuisson : 5 min**

16 gambas • 2 cuil. à soupe d'huile d'olive • ½ citron vert • 1 cuil. à soupe de graines de coriandre • 8 brins de coriandre fraîche • sel, poivre

Réalisation

Pressez le demi-citron vert, versez le jus dans un plat creux, ajoutez l'huile, les graines de coriandre concassées, du sel et du poivre. Décortiquez les gambas, mettez-les au fur et à mesure dans cette marinade.

Faites chauffer une poêle, versez les gambas avec leur marinade, faites cuire à feu vif pendant 5 minutes en mélangeant.

Répartissez sur quatre petites assiettes, parsemez de brins de coriandre ciselés.

HADDOCK EN SALADE À L'ORANGE

4 pers. **Préparation : 15 min** **Cuisson : 10 min**

600 g de haddock • 10 cl de lait • 1 salade feuille de chêne
• 1 orange • 1 cuil. à soupe de vinaigre de cidre • 1 cuil.
à café de moutarde • 4 cuil. à soupe d'huile de colza
• sel, poivre

Réalisation

Coupez le haddock en lamelles. Placez-le dans une casserole, versez-y le lait, complétez d'eau pour que le poisson soit recouvert. Portez à ébullition et laissez pocher pendant 10 minutes.

Pendant ce temps, lavez et essorez la salade, mettez-la dans un saladier. Pressez l'orange. Préparez la sauce en mélangeant la moutarde, le vinaigre, l'huile, du sel, du poivre et le jus d'orange.

Égouttez le haddock, déposez-le sur la salade, arrosez de sauce. Servez aussitôt.

HADDOCK ET CHOU CHINOIS EN SALADE ⏱

4 pers.   **Préparation : 10 min**

½ chou chinois • 200 g de haddock • 2 pommes vertes • 15 cl de crème liquide • 2 citrons • sel, poivre

Réalisation

Pressez les citrons. Coupez le haddock en fines lamelles, arrosez-le de jus de citron. Émincez le chou. Épluchez les pommes, coupez-les en lamelles, citronnez-les.

Répartissez les ingrédients sur quatre assiettes, arrosez de crème, salez peu, poivrez généreusement. Servez frais.

LOTTE À LA PANCETTA ET AUX CÂPRES

4 pers. **Préparation : 10 min** **Cuisson : 10 min**

600 g de lotte • 8 tranches fines de pancetta • 2 cuil. à soupe d'huile d'olive • 2 gousses d'ail • 2 cuil. à soupe de câpres • sel, poivre

Réalisation

Coupez la lotte en gros dés et la pancetta en lanières. Pelez et écrasez l'ail.

Faites chauffer l'huile dans une sauteuse, mettez les dés de poisson, l'ail, faites-les dorer en les retournant régulièrement pendant 10 minutes, salez, poivrez.

Pendant ce temps, faites dorer à sec dans une poêle les morceaux de pancetta. Répartissez les dés de lotte et les morceaux de pancetta sur quatre assiettes, parsemez de câpres.

LOTTE AU CURRY

4 pers. **Préparation : 10 min** **Cuisson : 15 min**

600 g de lotte • 2 oignons • 1 yaourt nature • 2 cuil.
à soupe d'huile d'olive • 1 cuil. à soupe de pâte de curry
• sel, poivre

Réalisation

Pelez et hachez les oignons. Détaillez la lotte en dés.
Faites chauffer l'huile dans une sauteuse, faites dorer
les oignons pendant 5 minutes, puis ajoutez le poisson,
salez, poivrez, ajoutez la pâte de curry et le yaourt.
Mélangez, couvrez et laissez cuire pendant 5 minutes.
Répartissez dans quatre assiettes.

Notre conseil : servez avec du riz basmati nature et
du concombre raïta (concombre émincé dans du
yaourt).

MIJOTÉE DE POISSONS EXPRESS

4 pers. **Préparation : 15 min** **Cuisson : 5 min**

1 grand bocal de soupe de poisson • 400 g de poissons blancs • 4 tranches de pain de campagne • 2 cuil. à soupe d'huile d'olive • 1 gousse d'ail • ½ tomate • sel, poivre

Réalisation

Détaillez les poissons en petits dés. Versez la soupe de poisson dans une grande casserole, ajoutez les dés de poisson, faites chauffer et maintenez un petit frémissement pendant 5 minutes.

Pendant ce temps, pelez et écrasez l'ail, mettez-le dans un bol, ajoutez l'huile, salez et poivrez. Frottez les tranches de pain de campagne de tomate, puis badigeonnez-les d'huile à l'ail. Répartissez la mijotée dans des bols, servez avec les tartines.

Notre conseil : vous pouvez aussi couper le pain en dés, mettez-le dans la soupe, saupoudrez de gruyère râpé et passez sous le gril 5 minutes.

MOULES AU THYM

4 pers.   **Préparation : 5 min**   **Cuisson : 10 min**

2 litres de moules • 2 cuil. à soupe de thym effeuillé • 30 g
de beurre • 8 cl de vin blanc sec • sel, poivre

Réalisation

Lavez les moules, égouttez-les. Faites fondre le beurre
dans une grande sauteuse, ajoutez les moules, le thym,
salez, poivrez et arrosez de vin blanc. Faites sauter
à feu vif en secouant la sauteuse jusqu'à ce que les
moules soient toutes ouvertes.

Répartissez les moules dans quatre assiettes creuses
ou dans quatre petites cocottes individuelles. Servez
chaud.

PAVÉS DE LIEU COCO CURRY À LA CORIANDRE

4 pers. **Préparation : 5 min** **Cuisson : 15 min**

4 pavés de lieu • 20 cl de lait de coco • 6 branches de coriandre • 1 cuil. à café de curry • sel, poivre

Réalisation

Préchauffez le four à 210 °C (th. 7). Déposez les pavés de lieu dans un plat à four. Délayez le curry dans le lait de coco, versez sur le poisson, salez, poivrez. Enfournez et laissez cuire pendant 15 minutes. Parsemez de coriandre ciselée.

PETITS CALAMARS GRILLÉS

4 pers. **Préparation : 5 min** **Cuisson : 10 min**

600 g de petits calamars frais ou surgelés • 4 gousses d'ail • 100 g d'allumettes de lard fumé • 2 cuil. à soupe d'huile d'olive • 2 cuil. à soupe de vinaigre de xérès • sel, poivre

Réalisation

Pelez et écrasez l'ail. Faites chauffer l'huile dans une sauteuse, mettez les allumettes de lard et l'ail, faites dorer pendant 2 minutes puis ajoutez les calamars et prolongez la cuisson pendant 5 minutes en mélangeant.

Salez, poivrez, mélangez, versez sur le plat de service. Déglacez la sauteuse avec le vinaigre, versez sur les calamars. Servez aussitôt.

Notre conseil : servez avec des pâtes fraîches ou du riz.

ROUGETS AU BACON

4 pers. **Préparation : 10 min** **Cuisson : 5 min**

16 filets de rouget • 8 tranches de bacon • 2 cuil. à soupe d'huile d'olive • sel, poivre

Réalisation

Préchauffez le four à 210 °C (th. 7). Assemblez les filets de rouget deux par deux en intercalant une tranche de bacon.

Déposez-les dans un plat à four, arrosez d'un peu d'huile, salez peu, poivrez et laissez cuire pendant 5 à 8 minutes. Servez aussitôt.

ROUGETS TOMATES ET TAPENADE

4 pers. **Préparation : 10 min** **Cuisson : 10 min**

16 filets de rouget • 1 pot de tapenade • 3 tomates
• 2 branches de basilic • 1 cuil. à soupe d'huile

Réalisation

Préchauffez le four à 210 °C (th. 7). Badigeonnez d'huile un plat à four. Coupez les tomates en fines tranches, déposez-les au fond du plat. Tartinez les filets de rouget de tapenade, mettez-les sur les tomates.
Enfournez et laissez cuire pendant 10 minutes. Parsemez de feuilles de basilic ciselées. Servez bien chaud.

SAINT-JACQUES AUX HERBES ET AU PARMESAN

4 pers.   **Préparation : 10 min   Cuisson : 8 min**

16 noix de Saint-Jacques • 40 g de parmesan râpé • 30 g
de beurre • ½ botte de ciboulette • 2 pincées de piment
d'Espelette • 2 cuil. à soupe d'huile • sel

Réalisation

Ciselez finement la ciboulette, mélangez-la avec le beurre,
le parmesan râpé, le piment et un peu de sel.
Huilez un plat à four, déposez dans le plat les noix
de Saint-Jacques, tartinez-les de beurre aux herbes
et au parmesan et passez sous le gril pendant 5 à
8 minutes. Servez aussitôt.

Notre conseil : accompagnez ce plat d'une salade de
mesclun.

SAINT-JACQUES POÊLÉES AUX ÉCHALOTES

4 pers. **Préparation : 5 min** **Cuisson : 10 min**

20 noix de Saint-Jacques • 6 échalotes • 40 g de beurre
• sel, poivre du moulin

Réalisation

Pelez et émincez les échalotes. Faites chauffer le beurre
dans une poêle, faites fondre les échalotes à feu doux
pendant 5 minutes en mélangeant. Ajoutez les noix de
Saint-Jacques, retournez-les plusieurs fois, prolongez
la cuisson pendant 5 minutes. Salez, poivrez.
Répartissez sur quatre petites assiettes et servez
immédiatement.

Notre conseil : accompagnez de riz.

SALADE DE HARICOTS VERTS AU CRABE

4 pers.   **Préparation : 10 min**   **Cuisson : 10 min**

800 g de haricots verts frais ou surgelés • 400 g de chair de crabe • 1 bouquet de ciboulette • 1 citron • 1 cuil. à soupe de moutarde forte • 2 yaourts nature • sel, poivre

Réalisation

Faites cuire les haricots verts pendant 8 minutes dans de l'eau bouillante salée ; surveillez la cuisson pour qu'ils restent croquants. Égouttez-les, mettez-les dans un saladier. Ajoutez le crabe égoutté.

Pressez le citron, mélangez le jus avec la moutarde, les yaourts, du sel et du poivre. Versez sur la salade, mélangez et décorez de brins de ciboulette ciselés. Servez aussitôt.

Notre conseil : vous pouvez aussi servir cette salade froide.

SALADE DE LENTILLES AU THON ⏱

4 pers. **Préparation : 10 min**

500 g de lentilles cuites • 2 échalotes • 400 g de thon
au naturel • 1 cuil. à soupe de moutarde • 2 cuil. à soupe
de vinaigre de vin • 4 cuil. à soupe d'huile de colza
• 2 branches de persil • sel, poivre

Réalisation

Versez les lentilles dans un saladier, égouttez le thon,
ajoutez-le. Pelez et hachez les échalotes.

Préparez la sauce en battant la moutarde avec le
vinaigre, du sel, du poivre et l'huile versée en filet.
Arrosez la salade de sauce et parsemez de brins de
persil et d'échalotes hachées.

SALADE DE MÂCHE ET DE THON À L'ANANAS

4 pers. **Préparation : 15 min**

1 sachet de mâche • 400 g de thon au naturel • 1 petite boîte d'ananas au sirop • 2 échalotes • 4 cuil. à soupe de mayonnaise • 2 cuil. à soupe de ketchup • 4 gouttes de Tabasco

Réalisation

Rincez et essorez la mâche, répartissez-la sur quatre assiettes. Pelez et hachez les échalotes.

Mélangez dans un saladier la mayonnaise, le ketchup et le Tabasco. Égouttez le thon et les morceaux d'ananas, ajoutez-les, mélangez bien et répartissez sur la salade. Servez frais.

SALADE DE MÂCHE, SAUMON ET BAIES ROSES ⏱

4 pers. **Préparation : 10 min**

> 1 sachet de mâche • 600 g de saumon frais • 1 citron vert
> • 1 citron jaune • 10 cl de crème liquide • 4 cuil. à soupe
> d'huile d'olive • 2 cuil. à soupe de baies roses • 16 brins
> de ciboulette • sel, poivre

Réalisation

Lavez et essorez la mâche, répartissez-la sur quatre assiettes. Pressez les citrons, mélangez le jus obtenu dans un saladier avec la crème, l'huile, la ciboulette ciselée, du sel et du poivre.

Hachez grossièrement le saumon au couteau, mettez-le dans le saladier, mélangez bien, puis déposez-le sur la salade. Parsemez de baies roses. Servez bien frais.

SALADE DE POISSONS FUMÉS À L'OIGNON ROUGE

4 pers.   **Préparation : 15 min**

1 laitue • 200 g de saumon fumé • 300 g de truite fumée • 2 oignons rouges • 12 brins de ciboulette • ½ citron • 3 cuil. à soupe d'huile d'olive • sel, poivre

Réalisation

Rincez et essorez la laitue, mettez-la dans un saladier. Coupez les poissons en dés, ajoutez-les. Pelez les oignons, coupez-les en rondelles, détachez-les. Pressez le demi-citron, mélangez le jus avec l'huile, salez peu, poivrez, versez sur la salade. Ajoutez les oignons, décorez de ciboulette ciselée.

SALADE DE MANGUES, ROQUETTE ET CREVETTES

4 pers. **Préparation : 15 min**

12 à 20 crevettes roses cuites décortiquées • 2 mangues • 300 g de roquette • 2 petits oignons blancs • 1 citron vert • 4 gouttes de Tabasco • 3 cuil. à soupe de gingembre moulu • 4 cuil. à soupe d'huile de colza • sel, poivre

Pressez le citron, versez le jus dans un saladier, ajoutez le Tabasco, l'huile, du sel, du poivre et le gingembre. Pelez et hachez menu les oignons, ajoutez-les ainsi que les crevettes. Mélangez.

Pelez les mangues, retirez les noyaux et coupez la pulpe en dés. Lavez et essorez la roquette. Ajoutez-les dans le saladier, mélangez et répartissez dans quatre bols. Servez aussitôt.

Notre conseil : ajoutez la roquette juste au moment de servir si vous préparez cette salade un peu à l'avance, afin qu'elle ne fane pas.

SAUMON GRILLÉ ET POUSSES D'ÉPINARD

4 pers. **Préparation : 10 min** **Cuisson : 5 min**

4 pavés de saumon frais • 300 g de pousses d'épinard fraîches • 3 cuil. à soupe d'huile d'olive • 1 cuil. à soupe de vinaigre balsamique • 2 pincées de piment d'Espelette • sel

Réalisation

Coupez les pavés de saumon en deux dans l'épaisseur. Mettez-les dans un plat à four et passez sous le gril pendant 5 minutes.

Pendant ce temps, lavez les pousses d'épinard, séchez-les, mettez-les sur quatre assiettes.

Mélangez le vinaigre et l'huile avec un peu de sel et le piment, versez sur les pousses d'épinard. Déposez dessus des lamelles de poisson et servez aussitôt.

SAUMON PANÉ AUX HERBES

4 pers. **Préparation : 10 min** **Cuisson : 10 min**

4 pavés de saumon • 6 cuil. à soupe de chapelure • 2 branches de persil • 12 brins de ciboulette • 1 citron • 2 gousses d'ail • sel, poivre

Réalisation

Préchauffez le four à 210 °C (th. 7). Pressez le citron, pelez et écrasez l'ail, ciselez finement les herbes. Mélangez l'ail et le jus de citron avec la chapelure, les herbes, du sel et du poivre.

Enduisez les pavés de saumon avec cette préparation, déposez-les dans un plat à four et faites cuire pendant 10 minutes. Servez aussitôt.

TAGLIATELLES AU SAUMON, CURRY ET CORIANDRE

4 pers.   **Préparation : 10 min   Cuisson : 8 min**

> 200 g de saumon frais • 250 g de tagliatelles • 2 échalotes
> • 20 cl de crème liquide • 2 cuil. à soupe de curry • 1 cuil.
> à soupe d'huile d'arachide • ½ botte de coriandre • sel,
> poivre

Réalisation

Faites pocher le saumon dans de l'eau bouillante salée pendant 5 à 8 minutes selon l'épaisseur des morceaux. Faites cuire les tagliatelles dans de l'eau bouillante salée pendant 8 minutes.

Pendant ce temps, pelez les échalotes, hachez-les. Faites chauffer l'huile dans une sauteuse, faites revenir les échalotes, saupoudrez de curry, ajoutez la crème liquide, du sel, du poivre et laissez mijoter pendant 5 minutes.

Égouttez les pâtes, mettez-les dans un plat creux. Effilochez le saumon, disposez-le dessus et arrosez de sauce. Parsemez de coriandre ciselée.

TAGLIATELLES AUX CREVETTES

4 pers.   Préparation : 10 min   Cuisson : 15 min

250 g de tagliatelles • 2 oignons • 400 g de crevettes roses décortiquées • 8 cl de vin blanc sec • 20 cl de crème fraîche • 2 cuil. à soupe d'huile d'olive • sel, poivre

Réalisation

Faites bouillir de l'eau salée dans une grande casserole. Dès l'ébullition, jetez les tagliatelles, mélangez et laissez cuire pendant 10 minutes dès la reprise de l'ébullition.

Pelez et hachez les oignons. Faites chauffer l'huile dans une sauteuse, mettez les oignons, faites-les revenir pendant 2 minutes, puis ajoutez les crevettes, du sel, du poivre et le vin blanc.

Faites réduire à feu vif pendant 2 minutes, ajoutez la crème, mélangez. Égouttez les tagliatelles, versez-les dans un plat creux, arrosez de sauce aux crevettes. Servez aussitôt.

TAGLIATELLES AUX GAMBAS

4 pers.   **Préparation : 10 min**   **Cuisson : 10 min**

400 g de tagliatelles • 16 gambas • 2 cuil. à soupe d'huile d'olive • 1 orange • 100 g de beurre • 2 cuil. à soupe de gingembre moulu • sel, poivre du moulin

Réalisation

Faites cuire les tagliatelles dans une grande casserole d'eau bouillante salée pendant 10 minutes.

Pendant ce temps, pressez l'orange. Faites fondre le beurre dans une casserole, ajoutez le jus d'orange et le gingembre. Retirez du feu.

Faites chauffer l'huile dans une poêle, faites cuire les gambas pendant 5 minutes à feu vif en les retournant souvent. Égouttez les tagliatelles, versez-les dans un plat creux, arrosez de beurre à l'orange, déposez dessus les gambas et donnez un tour de moulin à poivre. Servez aussitôt.

TARTARE DE SAUMON AU GINGEMBRE

4 pers. **Préparation : 15 min**

600 g de saumon frais • 3 petits oignons blancs • 2 cm
de gingembre frais • 1 citron vert non traité • 4 cuil.
à soupe de sauce de soja • 2 cuil. à soupe d'huile de colza
• 12 brins de ciboulette

Réalisation

Pelez et hachez les oignons et le gingembre. Râpez le
zeste du citron, pressez le fruit. Hachez au couteau le
saumon, mettez-le dans un saladier, ajoutez le zeste
et le jus du citron, les oignons, le gingembre, la sauce
de soja et l'huile de colza.

Mélangez, vérifiez l'assaisonnement, rectifiez si nécessaire. Répartissez le tartare sur quatre petites assiettes,
décorez de brins de ciboulette. Servez bien frais.

VIANDES ET VOLAILLES RAPIDES

•

AIGUILLETTES DE CANARD AU POIVRE VERT

4 pers.   **Préparation : 5 min**   **Cuisson : 10 min**

600 g d'aiguillettes de canard • 2 cuil. à soupe de poivre vert • 20 cl de crème fraiche • 20 g de beurre • sel

Réalisation

Faites chauffer le beurre dans une poêle à revêtement antiadhésif, faites revenir les aiguillettes de canard pendant 5 minutes en les retournant souvent. Ajoutez le poivre vert, la crème, salez, laissez cuire encore 5 minutes. Servez aussitôt.

AIGUILLETTES DE CANARD MIEL ET NOIX

4 pers.   **Préparation : 10 min   Cuisson : 10 min**

800 g d'aiguillettes de canard • 2 échalotes • 12 cerneaux de noix concassés • 4 cuil. à soupe de miel • 1 cuil. à soupe de vinaigre de framboises • 2 cuil. à soupe d'huile d'olive • sel, poivre

Réalisation

Pelez et hachez les échalotes. Faites chauffer l'huile dans une poêle, faites revenir les échalotes pendant 3 minutes, ajoutez les aiguillettes, salez, poivrez et laissez cuire pendant 5 minutes.

Retirez-les avec une écumoire. Versez le miel et le vinaigre dans la poêle, ajoutez les noix concassées, portez à ébullition, remettez les aiguillettes, prolongez la cuisson pendant 1 minute pour les réchauffer. Servez aussitôt.

AIGUILLETTES DE POULET AU CURRY

4 pers. **Préparation : 10 min** **Cuisson : 15 min**

600 g de blanc de poulet • 1 poivron rouge • 1 oignon
• 10 cl de crème fraîche • 2 cuil. à soupe de curry • 2 cuil.
à soupe d'huile de tournesol • sel, poivre

Réalisation

Pelez et hachez l'oignon, détaillez le poivron rouge
en petits dés. Coupez le poulet en lamelles.

Faites chauffer l'huile dans une sauteuse, mettez
les oignons et les dés de poivron, faites revenir en
mélangeant pendant 3 minutes, ajoutez les lamelles de
poulet et prolongez la cuisson pendant 10 minutes.
Mélangez la crème et le curry, salez, poivrez, versez
dans la poêle et laissez cuire pendant 3 minutes,
servez aussitôt.

Notre conseil : accompagnez ce poulet de riz basmati.

BAVETTE AUX ÉCHALOTES

4 pers. **Préparation : 10 min   Cuisson : 10 min**

4 tranches de bœuf dans la bavette • 8 échalotes • 50 g de beurre • 1 cuil. à soupe de vinaigre de vin • sel, poivre

Réalisation

Pelez et émincez les échalotes. Faites fondre le beurre dans une poêle, mettez les échalotes, faites-les revenir pendant 5 à 8 minutes à feu moyen en mélangeant, salez, poivrez, déglacez avec le vinaigre et laissez-le évaporer. Réservez.

Faites griller les tranches de bavette pendant 3 à 5 minutes selon votre goût en les retournant à mi-cuisson.

Déposez la viande sur quatre assiettes, nappez d'échalotes et de sauce. Servez immédiatement.

BŒUF AUX LÉGUMES CROQUANTS À LA CORIANDRE

4 pers. Préparation : 15 min Cuisson : 15 min

400 g de bœuf (filet ou rumsteck) • 2 courgettes • 1 tête de brocoli • 1 poivron rouge • 3 cuil. à soupe d'huile d'olive • 40 cl de vin blanc sec • 3 cuil. à soupe de vinaigre de xérès • 1 botte de coriandre • sel, poivre

Réalisation

Détaillez la viande en fines lamelles. Séparez le brocoli en petits bouquets. Coupez les courgettes en rondelles et chaque rondelle en quatre. Coupez le poivron en dés après avoir retiré le pédoncule et les parties blanches.

Faites chauffer l'huile dans une sauteuse, mettez tous les légumes, salez, poivrez, arrosez de vin blanc, mélangez, couvrez et laissez cuire pendant 10 minutes en mélangeant de temps en temps.

Faites griller les lamelles de bœuf dans une poêle. Versez le vinaigre sur les légumes, disposez dans un plat creux, déposez la viande par-dessus et parsemez de coriandre ciselée.

BŒUF AUX OIGNONS ET AU GINGEMBRE

4 pers.   **Préparation : 10 min**   **Cuisson : 10 min**

600 g de bœuf (rumsteck ou faux-filet) • 4 oignons • 2 cuil. à soupe de sauce de soja • 2 cuil. à soupe de vinaigre blanc • 1 cuil. à café de sucre • 2 cuil. à soupe de gingembre moulu • 2 cuil. à soupe d'huile de tournesol • 2 cuil. à soupe de graines de sésame • poivre

Réalisation

Pelez et émincez les oignons. Coupez la viande en fines lamelles. Faites chauffer l'huile dans une sauteuse ou un wok, faites revenir les oignons en mélangeant pendant 2 minutes, saupoudrez de sucre et de gingembre, poivrez, arrosez de sauce de soja et de vinaigre. Poursuivez la cuisson jusqu'à ce que les oignons soient tendres.

Pendant ce temps, faites revenir les lamelles de viande dans une poêle très chaude en les retournant. Ajoutez la viande aux oignons, mélangez et répartissez dans quatre bols. Saupoudrez de graines de sésame. Servez aussitôt.

Nos conseils : accompagnez de riz. Faites griller les graines de sésame à sec dans une poêle, afin qu'elles dégagent tout leur parfum.

BŒUF SAUTÉ AU GINGEMBRE

4 pers. **Préparation : 10 min** **Cuisson : 10 min**

600 g de bœuf (filet ou rumsteck) • 6 cm de gingembre frais • 2 cuil. à soupe de gingembre en poudre • 2 gousses d'ail • 4 cuil. à soupe de sauce de soja • 1 citron vert • 2 cuil. à soupe de vinaigre de xérès • 2 cuil. à soupe d'huile d'arachide

Réalisation

Pelez le gingembre et hachez-le. Pelez les gousses d'ail, écrasez-les au-dessus d'un bol. Pressez le citron vert, versez le jus dans le bol, ajoutez le gingembre moulu, le gingembre haché, le vinaigre et la sauce soja. Détaillez le bœuf en lamelles. Faites chauffer l'huile dans une sauteuse ou un wok, faites revenir à feu vif la viande pendant 5 minutes, arrosez de sauce et prolongez la cuisson pendant 1 minute. Servez aussitôt.

BRICKS DE BŒUF AUX ÉPICES

4 pers. **Préparation : 10 min** **Cuisson : 15 min**

8 feuilles de brick • 400 g de bœuf haché • 2 oignons
• ½ bouquet de coriandre • 2 cuil. à soupe de cannelle
en poudre • 20 g de beurre • 2 cuil. à soupe d'huile d'olive
• sel, poivre

Réalisation

Pelez et hachez les oignons. Ciselez la coriandre.
Faites fondre le beurre dans une casserole. Faites
chauffer l'huile dans une poêle, faites dorer les
oignons, ajoutez le bœuf haché, du sel, du poivre,
la cannelle et les feuilles de coriandre. Mélangez et
laissez cuire pendant 5 minutes.
Préchauffez le four à 240 °C (th. 8). Étalez les feuilles
de brick en les superposant deux par deux. Répartissez
la viande sur les feuilles, repliez-les en triangles.
Badigeonnez-les de beurre fondu. Déposez-les sur
la plaque du four et faites dorer pendant 10 minutes
en les retournant délicatement à mi-cuisson. Servez
chaud ou tiède.

Nos conseils : accompagnez d'une salade de tomates au cumin et à l'huile d'olive. Vous pouvez aussi faire dorer les bricks à la poêle dans du beurre.

CANARD AU CURRY

4 pers. **Préparation : 5 min** **Cuisson : 10 min**

> 2 magrets de canard de 300 g chacun • 20 cl de lait de coco • 2 cuil. à soupe de gingembre moulu • 2 cuil. à soupe de curry doux • 3 cuil. à soupe d'huile de tournesol • sel, poivre

Réalisation

Ôtez la peau des magrets, coupez-les en fines tranches.

Faites chauffer l'huile dans un wok, faites sauter les tranches de canard pendant 2 minutes, salez, poivrez, saupoudrez de gingembre et de curry, arrosez de lait de coco et prolongez la cuisson pendant 4 à 5 minutes.

CUISSES DE CANARD CONFIT GRILLÉES AUX LENTILLES

4 pers.   **Préparation : 5 min**   **Cuisson : 10 min**

4 cuisses de canard confit • 1 boîte de lentilles à la graisse d'oie • 4 branches de persil

Réalisation

Déposez les cuisses de canard dans un plat à four. Passez-les sous le gril du four pendant 10 minutes en les retournant à mi-cuisson et en surveillant la couleur. La peau doit être brune et croustillante.

Pendant ce temps, faites réchauffer les lentilles dans leur jus dans une casserole. Répartissez les lentilles sur quatre assiettes, déposez sur chacune une cuisse de canard grillée et décorez de persil ciselé.

ÉMINCÉ D'AGNEAU AU BASILIC ⏲

4 pers. **Préparation : 5 min** **Cuisson : 5 min**

600 g d'épaule d'agneau • 2 gousses d'ail • 200 g de tomates confites • 4 branches de basilic • 3 cuil. à soupe d'huile d'olive • sel, poivre

Réalisation

Pelez et hachez l'ail. Détaillez l'agneau en lamelles. Faites chauffer l'huile dans une sauteuse, faites revenir les lamelles d'agneau avec l'ail à feu vif pendant 2 minutes en mélangeant, ajoutez les tomates confites et le basilic ciselé, salez et poivrez. Prolongez la cuisson pendant 3 minutes.

Notre conseil : servez avec des pâtes fraîches.

ÉMINCÉ DE BŒUF AU PAPRIKA

4 pers. **Préparation : 10 min**   **Cuisson : 5 min**

600 g de bœuf (filet ou rumsteck) • 3 échalotes • 1 cuil.
à soupe de paprika • 30 cl de crème fraîche • 20 g de
beurre • sel, poivre

Réalisation

Pelez et hachez les échalotes. Coupez la viande en
lamelles.
Faites fondre le beurre dans une poêle, faites revenir
les échalotes pendant 3 minutes puis ajoutez la viande,
prolongez la cuisson à feu vif pendant 1 minute,
saupoudrez de paprika, d'un peu de sel et de poivre
et versez la crème. Mélangez sur feu doux pendant
3 minutes. Servez aussitôt.

ÉMINCÉ DE BŒUF, SALADE DE ROQUETTE

4 pers. **Préparation : 10 min** **Cuisson : 3 min**

400 g de faux-filet de bœuf • 300 g de roquette • 1 cuil. à soupe de graines de sésame • 2 cuil. à soupe de vinaigre de xérès • 4 cuil. à soupe d'huile d'olive • sel, poivre du moulin

Réalisation

Coupez le bœuf en fines lamelles. Lavez et essorez la roquette, répartissez-la dans quatre coupelles. Préparez la sauce en mélangeant le vinaigre et l'huile avec un peu de sel et de poivre.

Faites griller les lamelles de viande sur un gril ou dans une poêle bien chaude pendant 2 à 3 minutes. Faites griller les graines de sésame à sec dans une poêle.

Déposez la viande sur la roquette, arrosez de sauce et parsemez de graines de sésame.

ESCALOPES DE DINDE AUX TOMATES CONFITES

4 pers.   **Préparation : 10 min**   **Cuisson : 10 min**

4 escalopes de dinde • 2 cuil. à soupe d'huile d'olive
• 8 tomates confites • 1 cuil. à soupe d'herbes de Provence
• 1 cuil. à soupe de vinaigre balsamique • sel, poivre

Réalisation

Coupez les tomates confites en morceaux. Faites chauffer l'huile dans une poêle, faites dorer les escalopes de dinde sur les deux faces et prolongez la cuisson pendant 10 minutes. Salez, poivrez, ajoutez les dés de tomate confite et les herbes.

Déposez les escalopes sur un plat, déglacez la poêle avec le vinaigre balsamique, versez la sauce sur la viande. Servez aussitôt.

ESCALOPES DE POULET AU PARMESAN

4 pers.   **Préparation : 10 min   Cuisson : 15 min**

4 escalopes de poulet très fines • 3 cuil. à soupe de farine
• 1 œuf • 60 g de parmesan râpé • 30 g de chapelure • 80 g
de beurre • sel, poivre

Réalisation

Versez la chapelure et le parmesan dans une assiette
creuse. Versez la farine dans une deuxième assiette,
et battez l'œuf dans une troisième, salez, poivrez.
Faites chauffer le beurre dans une grande poêle.
Trempez les escalopes successivement dans la farine,
l'œuf battu et le parmesan, déposez-les dans la poêle.
Faites cuire à feu doux pendant 7 minutes, retournez-
les et poursuivez la cuisson pendant 7 minutes. Servez
immédiatement.

Notre conseil : accompagnez de rondelles de citron.

ESCALOPES DE VEAU GRATINÉES

4 pers.   **Préparation : 5 min**   **Cuisson : 15 min**

4 escalopes de veau larges et fines • 4 tranches de jambon cru • 50 g de parmesan râpé • 1 cuil. à soupe de sauge séchée • 20 g de beurre • 2 cuil. à soupe d'huile d'olive • sel, poivre

Réalisation

Faites chauffer l'huile et le beurre dans une grande poêle. Faites dorer les escalopes de veau sur les deux faces pendant 5 minutes, puis placez-les dans un plat à four.

Mettez sur chacune d'elles une tranche de jambon, un peu de parmesan et de la sauge, salez, poivrez. Versez le jus de cuisson et passez sous le gril pendant 5 minutes en surveillant la couleur.

Notre conseil : accompagnez de polenta.

FAUX FILET À LA THAÏE

4 pers. **Préparation : 10 min** **Cuisson : 5 min**

2 tranches de faux filet • 4 branches de menthe • ½ bouquet de coriandre • 12 brins de ciboulette • 2 petits oignons • 4 cuil. à soupe de cacahuètes nature • 3 cuil. à soupe d'huile • 2 cuil. à soupe de sauce de soja • 2 cuil. à soupe de gingembre moulu

Réalisation

Pelez et hachez les petits oignons, mettez-les dans un grand bol, ajoutez l'huile, la sauce de soja et le gingembre. Faites griller les cacahuètes à sec dans une poêle, concassez-les grossièrement. Détachez les feuilles de menthe puis ciselez-les avec la coriandre et la ciboulette.

Faites cuire les tranches de faux filet dans une poêle bien chaude pendant 2 à 3 minutes sur chaque face selon l'épaisseur des tranches et votre goût. Coupez les tranches en deux, disposez-les sur les assiettes, recouvrez-les d'herbes ciselées, parsemez de cacahuètes grillées et arrosez de sauce. Servez immédiatement.

FOIE DE VEAU, CARAMEL AU CITRON

4 pers.   **Préparation : 5 min**   **Cuisson : 15 min**

4 tranches de foie de veau • 2 oignons • 8 cl de vin blanc
sec • 2 cuil. à soupe de poivre concassé • 2 cuil. à soupe
de miel liquide • 30 g de beurre • ½ citron • sel

Réalisation

Pelez et hachez les oignons. Coupez les tranches de
foie en lanières. Pressez le demi-citron.

Faites chauffer le beurre dans une grande poêle, faites
revenir les oignons pendant 3 minutes, puis ajoutez
les lanières de foie et poursuivez la cuisson pendant
5 à 8 minutes. Retirez le foie et les oignons. Versez le
vin blanc, laissez-le réduire pendant 1 minute, puis
ajoutez le miel et le poivre, mélangez pour obtenir
un caramel blond, arrosez de jus de citron.

Remettez le foie et les oignons, salez, mélangez
avec la sauce, laissez réchauffer 1 minute et servez
aussitôt.

Notre conseil : accompagnez de purée de pommes de
terre ou de pâtes fraîches.

FRICASSÉE DE POULET AUX FRUITS SECS

4 pers. **Préparation : 10 min** **Cuisson : 15 min**

600 g de blancs de poulet • 8 abricots secs • 2 cuil. à soupe de miel • 40 cl de crème liquide • 2 cuil. à soupe d'huile d'olive • 50 g de pistaches non salées • sel, poivre

Réalisation

Concassez grossièrement les pistaches. Coupez les blancs de poulet et les abricots en lamelles fines.

Faites chauffer l'huile dans une sauteuse, faites dorer les lamelles de poulet en les retournant plusieurs fois pendant 5 minutes, puis retirez-les. Versez le miel dans la sauteuse, grattez avec une cuillère en bois pour décoller les sucs de cuisson et versez la crème, salez, poivrez, mélangez.

Dès que la crème frémit, ajoutez les abricots, laissez cuire pendant 5 minutes, puis remettez les lamelles de viande. Réchauffez pendant 3 minutes. Parsemez de pistaches concassées et servez bien chaud.

GRILLADES DE GIGOT D'AGNEAU À LA FLEUR DE THYM ⏲

4 pers.   **Préparation : 5 min**   **Cuisson : 5 min**

> 4 tranches d'agneau dans le gigot • 2 cuil. à soupe de thym effeuillé • sel, poivre

Réalisation

Mélangez dans une assiette creuse le thym, du sel et du poivre. Faites chauffer une poêle. Passez les tranches de gigot dans les herbes et faites-les cuire à feu vif pendant 5 minutes en les retournant à mi-cuisson. Déposez sur les assiettes et servez immédiatement.

Notre conseil : accompagnez de tomates poêlées et/ou de flageolets verts.

JAMBON AU POIVRE ⏱

4 pers   **Préparation : 5 min   Cuisson : 5 min**

4 tranches de jambon à l'os • 20 cl de crème fraîche • 20 g de beurre • 4 cuil. à soupe de poivre concassé • sel

Réalisation

Mélangez le poivre et la crème avec un peu de sel. Faites fondre le beurre dans une poêle, faites dorer légèrement les tranches de jambon pendant 3 minutes, puis versez la crème assaisonnée. Prolongez la cuisson pendant 2 minutes. Servez bien chaud.

Notre conseil : accompagnez d'épinards au beurre.

LAMELLES DE PORC À L'ANANAS

4 pers.   **Préparation : 10 min   Cuisson : 10 min**

600 g de filet de porc • 1 boîte d'ananas en morceaux au sirop • 2 cuil. à soupe de gingembre moulu • 3 cuil. à soupe de sauce de soja • 4 pincées de piment en poudre • 1 cuil. à soupe de miel • 2 cuil. à soupe d'huile d'arachide

Réalisation

Coupez la viande en fines lamelles. Égouttez les morceaux d'ananas en conservant le sirop. Mélangez dans un bol le miel avec le gingembre, le piment, la sauce soja et quatre cuillerées à soupe du sirop d'ananas.

Faites chauffer l'huile dans une sauteuse, faites revenir les lamelles de porc à feu moyen en les retournant régulièrement pendant 5 minutes, puis versez la sauce, ajoutez les morceaux d'ananas, mélangez, couvrez et laissez cuire encore 5 minutes à feu doux.

HACHIS DE BŒUF PIMENTÉ AU BASILIC ⏱

4 pers. **Préparation : 5 min** **Cuisson : 5 min**

600 g de bœuf haché • 1 piment oiseau • 3 cuil. à soupe d'huile de tournesol • 4 branches de basilic • 12 feuilles de laitue • sel, poivre

Réalisation

Ciselez les feuilles de laitue, répartissez-les dans quatre bols. Ciselez les feuilles de basilic.

Faites chauffer l'huile dans une sauteuse ou un wok, ajoutez la viande ha____ émiettez le piment oiseau ____ sans cesser de mélanger ____

S____ silic ciselé. Poursuivez la cu____ ez dans les bols.

PÂTES FRAÎCHES À LA SAUGE, COPPA GRILLÉE

4 pers.   **Préparation : 5 min**   **Cuisson : 10 min**

350 g de pâtes fraîches • 16 tranches de coppa • 100 g de beurre • 10 feuilles de sauge • 100 g de parmesan • sel, poivre

Réalisation

Faites griller les tranches de coppa pendant 3 minutes à sec dans une poêle. Faites cuire les pâtes pendant 3 minutes dans de l'eau bouillante salée.

Faites fondre le beurre dans une casserole, ajoutez les feuilles de sauge ciselées, du sel et du poivre.

Égouttez les pâtes, versez-les dans un plat creux, arrosez de beurre, déposez dessus les tranches de coppa et saupoudrez de parmesan. Servez bien chaud.

PAVÉS DE BŒUF, CRÈME DE BAIES ROSES

4 pers. **Préparation : 5 min** **Cuisson : 10 min**

4 pavés de bœuf • 4 cl de vin blanc sec • 15 cl de crème fraîche • 2 cuil. à soupe de baies roses • sel, poivre

Réalisation

Versez le vin blanc dans une casserole, ajoutez les baies roses et portez à ébullition. Faites réduire de moitié, puis ajoutez la crème, salez et poivrez. Réservez. Faites griller les pavés de bœuf, déposez-les sur des assiettes, nappez de sauce et servez immédiatement.

PETITS PILONS DE POULET AU MIEL

4 pers. **Préparation : 5 min** **Cuisson : 15 min**

12 petits pilons de poulet • 3 cuil. à soupe de miel • 4 cuil. à soupe de vinaigre balsamique • 1 cuil. à soupe de paprika • 3 cuil. à soupe d'huile de tournesol • sel, poivre

Réalisation

Faites chauffer l'huile dans une sauteuse, faites revenir les pilons en les retournant pour qu'ils soient dorés de tous côtés, salez, poivrez et laissez cuire pendant 10 minutes.

Délayez le miel dans le vinaigre, ajoutez le paprika, du sel et du poivre. Versez dans la sauteuse, mélangez pour que les pilons soient bien enrobés, laissez caraméliser pendant 5 minutes. Servez bien chaud.

POULET AU SÉSAME

4 pers.   **Préparation : 5 min**   **Cuisson : 15 min**

> 600 g de blancs de poulet • 4 cm de gingembre frais • 4 gousses d'ail • 6 cuil. à soupe de sauce de soja • 3 cuil. à soupe d'huile d'arachide • 4 cuil. à soupe de graines de sésame

Réalisation

Émincez le poulet en lamelles. Pelez et émincez le gingembre et les gousses d'ail.

Faites chauffer l'huile dans une sauteuse ou un wok, faites revenir les lamelles de gingembre et d'ail pendant 3 minutes sans cesser de mélanger, ajoutez les lamelles de poulet, poursuivez la cuisson pendant 8 à 10 minutes en les retournant régulièrement.

Arrosez de sauce de soja, faites réduire un peu puis saupoudrez de sésame en retournant les lamelles pour qu'elles soient bien enrobées. Servez immédiatement.

POULET AUX NOUILLES CHINOISES

4 pers.   **Préparation : 10 min**   **Cuisson : 15 min**

600 g de blancs de poulet • 2 oignons • 2 gousses d'ail • 250 g de nouilles chinoises • 2 cuil. à soupe de gingembre moulu • 4 cuil. à soupe de sauce de soja • 3 cuil. à soupe d'huile de tournesol

Réalisation

Pelez et hachez les oignons et les gousses d'ail. Coupez le poulet en lamelles.

Faites chauffer l'huile dans une sauteuse ou dans un wok, mettez l'ail et l'oignon, faites-les revenir, puis ajoutez les lamelles de poulet, saupoudrez de gingembre, arrosez de 4 cl d'eau, mélangez et laissez cuire pendant 10 minutes.

Pendant ce temps, faites cuire les nouilles dans de l'eau bouillante salée additionnée d'un filet d'huile pendant 5 minutes. Égouttez-les et mettez-les dans le wok. Versez la sauce de soja, mélangez et répartissez dans quatre bols. Servez bien chaud.

POULET COCO CORIANDRE

4 pers.   **Préparation : 10 min**   **Cuisson : 10 min**

4 blancs de poulet • 1 gros bouquet de coriandre • 1 brique de lait de coco • 2 cuil. à soupe d'huile d'olive • 1 cuil. à soupe de curry doux • sel, poivre

Réalisation

Coupez le poulet en lanières. Hachez la coriandre. Faites chauffer l'huile dans une sauteuse, faites revenir le poulet, salez, poivrez, ajoutez le curry, la coriandre hachée et arrosez de lait de coco.

Faites cuire à petits frémissements pendant 10 minutes. Servez chaud.

POULET CRÈME ESTRAGON

4 pers. **Préparation : 5 min** **Cuisson : 15 min**

4 blancs de poulet • 4 branches d'estragon • 20 cl de crème fraîche • 1 cuil. à café de moutarde forte • 30 g de beurre • sel, poivre

Réalisation

Coupez les blancs de poulet en lanières. Ciselez finement l'estragon. Faites fondre le beurre dans une sauteuse, faites dorer le poulet pendant 5 à 8 minutes en mélangeant souvent, salez, poivrez.

Mélangez la moutarde, la crème et l'estragon, versez sur le poulet. Prolongez la cuisson pendant 2 à 5 minutes. Servez aussitôt.

POULET TANDOORI, RIZ BASMATI

4 pers.   **Préparation : 5 min   Cuisson : 10 min**

4 blancs de poulet • 250 g de riz basmati • 1 oignon • 1 sachet
d'épices tandoori en poudre • 25 cl de crème liquide • 2 cuil.
à soupe d'huile de tournesol • sel, poivre

Réalisation

Faites chauffer de l'eau dans une grande casserole. Dès
l'ébullition, plongez le riz et laissez-le cuire pendant
8 à 10 minutes. Pelez et hachez l'oignon. Détaillez
les blancs de poulet en lamelles.

Faites chauffer l'huile dans une poêle, faites revenir
l'oignon pendant 3 minutes, puis ajoutez le poulet.
Faites cuire en mélangeant souvent pendant 5 minutes,
saupoudrez d'épices et arrosez de crème. Mélangez
et laissez cuire encore 3 minutes. Vérifiez l'assaisonnement, rectifiez si nécessaire.

Égouttez le riz, versez-le dans un plat creux, disposez
le poulet dessus. Servez chaud.

RÔTI DE MAGRETS À L'ORANGE ET AU MIEL

4 pers. **Préparation : 10 min** **Cuisson : 15 min**

2 magrets de canard de 300 g chacun • 1 orange • 3 cuil.
à soupe de miel • 2 cuil. à soupe d'huile d'olive • 4 cl
de fond de veau • sel, poivre

Réalisation

Préchauffez le four à 240 °C (th. 8). Lavez et essuyez
l'orange, coupez-la en tranches fines en récupérant
le jus de la découpe. Faites des entailles dans la peau
des magrets avec un bon couteau, salez, poivrez et
badigeonnez d'huile d'olive. Enduisez le côté chair
des magrets de miel, déposez dessus les tranches
d'orange et réunissez les magrets en les ficelant.

Déposez ce « rôti » dans un plat à four, arrosez de
fond de veau, ajoutez le jus d'orange de la découpe et
faites cuire pendant 10 à 15 minutes selon l'épaisseur
des magrets. Retirez la ficelle, tranchez les magrets
et répartissez-les sur quatre assiettes. Nappez de
sauce.

SALADE ALSACIENNE

4 pers.   **Préparation : 15 min**

2 petits cervelas cuits • 200 g de comté • 2 cœurs de sucrine • 2 échalotes • 6 cornichons • 1 cuil. à café de moutarde forte • 1 cuil. à soupe de vinaigre de vin • 4 cuil. à soupe d'huile de colza • 3 branches de persil • sel, poivre

Réalisation

Détaillez le fromage en bâtonnets. Pelez et émincez les échalotes. Coupez le cervelas et les cornichons en rondelles fines. Lavez et essorez la salade, coupez-la en lanières.

Mélangez dans un saladier la moutarde avec le vinaigre, un peu de sel et de poivre et l'huile. Ajoutez tous les ingrédients, et parsemez de persil ciselé. Mélangez au moment de servir.

SALADE D'ENDIVES, JAMBON, ROQUEFORT ET NOIX ⏲

4 pers. **Préparation : 10 min**

4 endives • 300 g d'allumettes de jambon • 50 g de roquefort • 100 g de cerneaux de noix • 1 cuil. à café de moutarde forte • 2 cuil. à soupe de vinaigre de vin • 5 cuil. à soupe d'huile de noix • poivre

Réalisation

Retirez les feuilles flétries des endives et coupez les autres en lamelles. Mettez-les dans un saladier, ajoutez les allumettes de jambon et les cerneaux de noix concassés.

Écrasez le roquefort dans un bol, ajoutez la moutarde, du poivre, le vinaigre et l'huile. Versez sur la salade, mélangez.

SALADE DE MAGRETS DE CANARD AUX MARRONS

4 pers.   Préparation : 15 min   Cuisson : 15 min

2 magrets de canards de 300 g chacun • 200 g de marrons au naturel • 1 sachet de mâche • 1 cuil. à soupe de moutarde forte • 2 cuil. à soupe de vinaigre de vin • 4 cuil. à soupe d'huile de noix • sel, poivre

Réalisation

Rincez et essorez la mâche, mettez-la dans un saladier. Préparez la vinaigrette : fouettez la moutarde avec le vinaigre, du sel et du poivre, et versez l'huile en filet. Réservez.

Réchauffez les marrons à feu doux dans une casserole. Faites chauffer une poêle, mettez les magrets côté peau, faites cuire à feu vif pendant 7 minutes, puis retournez-les et prolongez la cuisson pendant 7 minutes. Retirez les magrets, coupez-les en lamelles. Déposez les tranches de magret et les marrons sur la mâche, arrosez de sauce. Servez aussitôt.

TARTARE ALLER-RETOUR AUX HERBES ⏲

4 pers. **Préparation : 5 min** **Cuisson : 5 min**

4 steaks hachés • 4 petits oignons blancs nouveaux • 1 bouquet de cerfeuil • 4 brins de persil plat • 6 brins de ciboulette • 2 cuil. à soupe d'huile d'olive • sel, poivre

Réalisation

Ciselez les herbes et les oignons. Faites chauffer l'huile dans une poêle à revêtement antiadhésif. Faites dorer les steaks hachés pendant 2 minutes sur chaque côté, déposez-les sur les assiettes, salez, poivrez et recouvrez avec les herbes et les oignons. Servez immédiatement.

Notre conseil : accompagnez d'une purée de pommes de terre ou de haricots verts vapeur.

TARTARE CLASSIQUE ⏱

4 pers.   **Préparation : 10 min**

600 g de bœuf haché • 2 oignons • 2 cuil. à soupe de câpres • 2 jaunes d'œufs • ½ bouquet de persil • 4 cuil. à soupe de ketchup • 4 cuil. à soupe de Worcestershire sauce • 2 cuil. à soupe d'huile de colza • 2 cuil. à soupe de moutarde forte • sel, poivre

Réalisation

Pelez et hachez les oignons. Mettez la viande dans un grand saladier. Ajoutez les jaunes d'œufs, du sel, du poivre, les sauces, la moutarde, l'huile et les câpres. Mélangez à la fourchette.

Goûtez pour vérifier l'assaisonnement, rectifiez si nécessaire. Parsemez de feuilles de persil ciselées. Réservez au frais en attendant de servir.

Notre conseil : vous pouvez ajouter des cornichons coupés en petits dés.

TARTARE THAÏ ⏱

4 pers. **Préparation : 10 min**

600 g de bœuf haché • 2 oignons • 2 cuil. à soupe de
gingembre en poudre • 2 jaunes d'œufs • 4 cuil. à soupe
de sauce de soja • 1 cuil. à café de vinaigre blanc • 2 cuil.
à soupe de ketchup • ½ cuil. à café de purée de piment
• 1 botte de coriandre • 8 brins de ciboulette

Réalisation

Pelez et hachez les oignons. Ciselez finement la
coriandre et la ciboulette. Mettez la viande et les
oignons dans un saladier, ajoutez les jaunes d'œufs, les
sauces, le vinaigre, les épices et les herbes. Mélangez
bien et réservez au frais en attendant de servir.

DESSERTS VITE PRÊTS

•

ANANAS SAUTÉ À LA MENTHE

4 pers. **Préparation : 10 min** **Cuisson : 5 min**

1 ananas Victoria • 6 branches de menthe

Réalisation

Pelez l'ananas, retirez la partie fibreuse du centre et coupez la chair en dés. Faites chauffer une sauteuse ou un wok, mettez les dés d'ananas, laissez cuire à feu vif pendant 5 minutes, versez dans des coupes, parsemez de feuilles de menthe hachée.

Notre conseil : vous pouvez arroser les morceaux d'ananas d'un peu de rhum blanc 1 minute avant la fin de la cuisson.

BANANES COCO RHUM

4 pers.   **Préparation : 5 min**   **Cuisson : 10 min**

4 grosses bananes • 60 g de cassonade • 5 cl de lait de coco • 2 cuil. à soupe de rhum brun

Réalisation

Versez le lait de coco dans une casserole, ajoutez la cassonade, portez à ébullition. Préchauffez le four à 210 °C (th. 7).

Pelez les bananes, déposez chacune d'elles sur une feuille de papier sulfurisé, versez un peu de sirop, quelques gouttes de rhum, fermez les papillotes.

Déposez-les dans un plat à four et faites cuire pendant 10 minutes. Servez chaud ou tiède.

BOUCHÉES SABLÉES AUX FRAMBOISES ⏱

4 pers. **Préparation : 5 min**

12 biscuits sablés ronds • 36 framboises • 1 bombe de crème chantilly • 4 cuil. à soupe de sucre glace

Réalisation

Étalez un peu de crème chantilly sur chaque sablé, déposez dessus trois framboises. Mettez trois sablés par assiette et servez.

Notre conseil : variez les plaisirs en remplaçant les framboises par des petites fraises mara des bois.

CHANTILLY ORANGE CACAO ⏱

4 pers. **Préparation : 5 min**

1 bombe de crème chantilly • 2 cuil. à soupe de cacao amer • 6 zestes d'orange confite

Réalisation

Garnissez quatre verres de chantilly, poudrez de cacao. Coupez les zestes d'orange en petits dés, déposez-les dessus. Servez très frais.

COMPOTE DE CERISES AUX AMANDES

4 pers.   **Préparation : 10 min**   **Cuisson : 15 min**

800 g de cerises • 100 g de sucre • 50 g d'amandes mondées
• 1 gousse de vanille

Réalisation

Lavez rapidement les cerises, équeutez-les.

Versez 10 cl d'eau dans une casserole, ajoutez le sucre
et la gousse de vanille coupée en deux. Portez à
ébullition. Ajoutez les cerises et les amandes. Laissez
cuire 10 minutes à feu vif.

Le jus doit être sirupeux. Laissez refroidir et répartissez
dans quatre coupes. Mettez au frais.

Notre conseil : vous pouvez aromatiser cette compote
avec deux cuillerées à soupe de kirsch avant de
servir.

COMPOTE DE FRUITS ROUGES

4 pers. **Préparation : 5 min**   **Cuisson : 8 min**

400 g de fruits rouges surgelés • 50 g de beurre • 50 g de sucre • 2 cuil. à soupe de gingembre moulu

Réalisation

Faites fondre le beurre dans une casserole, ajoutez le sucre et le gingembre, mélangez à feu doux jusqu'à ce que le sucre soit fondu.

Ajoutez les fruits rouges, laissez cuire pendant 5 minutes en mélangeant. Versez dans quatre coupes. Servez tiède ou froid.

Notre conseil : servez nature, ou avec de la glace à la vanille et/ou des petits gâteaux moelleux aux noisettes (recette p. 142).

CRÈME AU CHOCOLAT ET PRALIN

4 pers.   **Préparation : 5 min**   **Cuisson : 10 min**

100 g de chocolat noir • 50 cl de lait • 30 g de fécule de maïs • 20 g de cassonade • 2 cuil. à café de pralin

Réalisation

Mettez la fécule dans un bol, délayez-la avec 10 cl de lait, ajoutez la cassonade, mélangez. Faites bouillir le reste de lait dans une casserole, retirez du feu, ajoutez le chocolat coupé en petits morceaux. Laissez-le fondre, mélangez puis versez la fécule délayée. Remettez sur le feu, portez à ébullition sans cesser de mélanger. Laissez cuire pendant 2 minutes, puis versez dans quatre ramequins. Laissez refroidir à température ambiante, puis mettez au frais en attendant de servir. Au dernier moment, saupoudrez de pralin.

CRÈME DE MARRONS AU CHOCOLAT ⏱

4 pers. **Préparation : 10 min**

400 g de crème de marrons • 10 cl de crème liquide • 100 g de chocolat noir • 4 cuil. à soupe de crème chantilly • 4 marrons glacés

Réalisation

Fouettez dans une terrine la crème de marrons avec la crème liquide. Versez dans quatre verres. Recouvrez de chantilly.

Faites fondre le chocolat au micro-ondes, versez-le sur la crème et déposez un marron glacé sur chaque verre.

CRUMBLES EXPRESS AUX POMMES

4 pers.   **Préparation : 5 min**   **Cuisson : 20 min**

600 g de compote de pommes sans sucre ajouté • 100 g de flocons d'avoine • 150 g de cassonade • 150 g de beurre • 1 cuil. à soupe de cannelle • sel

Réalisation

Répartissez la compote dans quatre petits plats à four individuels. Dans un saladier, travaillez du bout des doigts le beurre avec les flocons d'avoine, la cassonade, la cannelle et une pincée de sel pour obtenir une pâte sableuse.

Émiettez cette pâte sur la compote et enfournez. Laissez cuire pendant environ 20 minutes, jusqu'à ce que la pâte soit dorée. Laissez tiédir avant de servir.

Notre conseil : faites cuire les crumbles pendant le repas, sortez-les du four au moment du fromage, ils seront à la bonne température au dessert.

FIGUES À LA BROUSSE, MIEL ET CANNELLE ⏲

4 pers. **Préparation : 5 min**

4 figues fraîches • 4 figues sèches • 200 g de brousse • 2 cuil. à soupe de miel • 1 cuil. à soupe de cannelle

Réalisation

Coupez les figues sèches en très petits dés, mélangez-les à la brousse avec la cannelle et le miel. Ouvrez les figues fraîches en quatre sans les séparer, déposez au centre une grosse cuillerée à soupe de brousse. Déposez-les dans quatre verres et servez frais.

FIGUES RÔTIES AU CARAMEL SALÉ

4 pers. **Préparation : 15 min** **Cuisson : 10 min**

8 à 12 figues fraîches • 80 g de cassonade • 60 g de beurre demi-sel • 20 cl de crème fraîche • ½ citron

Réalisation

Préchauffez le four à 210 °C (th. 7). Lavez et essuyez les figues, coupez-les en quatre sans détacher les quartiers, déposez-les dans un plat à four, mettez au centre de chacune une noisette de beurre, saupoudrez d'une cuillerée à café de cassonade et faites cuire au four pendant 10 minutes.

Pendant ce temps, versez le reste de sucre dans une casserole, ajoutez 40 cl d'eau et le jus du demi-citron. Faites chauffer à feu vif pour obtenir un caramel ambré, ajoutez le reste de beurre, laissez fondre en mélangeant puis incorporez la crème. Nappez les figues de caramel et servez aussitôt.

Notre conseil : accompagnez ces figues rôties d'une boule de glace vanille.

FIGUES SÈCHES POCHÉES AU MIEL, GLACE VANILLE

4 pers. **Préparation : 5 min** **Cuisson : 15 min**

4 figues sèches • 4 cuil. à soupe de miel • 2 cuil. à soupe de noix de muscade râpée • 4 boules de glace vanille

Réalisation

Versez le miel dans une casserole, ajoutez 4 cl d'eau chaude et la noix de muscade. Portez à ébullition, baissez le feu et plongez les figues dans l'eau parfumée. Laissez cuire pendant 10 minutes en les retournant souvent.

Mettez une boule de glace vanille dans quatre verres. Répartissez les figues dans les verres, faites réduire le jus de cuisson à feu vif, versez sur les fruits. Servez aussitôt.

FRAMBOISES, MOUSSE DE FROMAGE BLANC ET BISCUITS ROSES ⏲

4 pers. **Préparation : 10 min**

1 paquet de biscuits roses de Reims • 400 g de framboises • 400 g de fromage blanc • 125 g de mascarpone • 4 boules de glace framboise • 2 cuil. à soupe de sucre glace

Réalisation

Fouettez le fromage blanc avec le mascarpone. Déposez dans quatre coupes une boule de glace, nappez de mousse au fromage blanc, émiettez quelques biscuits roses, ajoutez des framboises et saupoudrez d'un peu de sucre glace. Servez glacé.

GÂTEAU AU CHOCOLAT TGV

4 pers.   **Préparation : 10 min**   **Cuisson : 10 min**

150 g de chocolat noir • 2 œufs • 20 g de beurre + 20 g pour les moules • 20 g de sucre • sel

Réalisation

Préchauffez le four à 240 °C (th. 8). Beurrez quatre moules individuels. Cassez le chocolat en petits morceaux, mettez-le dans un grand bol avec le beurre et faites fondre au micro-ondes. Cassez les œufs en séparant les blancs des jaunes. Ajoutez au chocolat le sucre et les jaunes d'œufs.

Battez les œufs en neige avec une pincée de sel, incorporez-les au mélange. Répartissez dans les moules et enfournez. Laissez cuire pendant 5 minutes, puis recouvrez d'une feuille d'aluminium pour que les gâteaux cuisent sans brûler. Démoulez et laissez tiédir avant de déguster.

GLACE EN ROBE ⏱

4 pers. **Préparation : 10 min**

8 boules de glace vanille • 6 cuil. à soupe de cacao non sucré • 6 cuil. à soupe de noix de coco râpée

Réalisation

Versez le cacao dans une assiette creuse, et la noix de coco dans une seconde assiette. Roulez quatre boules de glace dans le cacao, et quatre boules de glace dans la noix de coco.

Déposez sur chaque assiette une boule au cacao, une boule à la noix de coco. Servez aussitôt.

LITCHIS À LA ROSE ⏱

4 pers. **Préparation : 5 min**

1 boîte de litchis au sirop • 2 cuil. à soupe d'eau de rose • 4 pétales de rose cristallisées

Réalisation

Égouttez les litchis en conservant le sirop. Répartissez-les dans quatre verres.

Mélangez le sirop avec l'eau de roses, versez sur les fruits et décorez d'un pétale de rose. Servez aussitôt.

Notre conseil : préparez le dessert avant le repas, placez au réfrigérateur et déposez les pétales au moment de servir pour que le sucre ne fonde pas au contact du sirop.

MOELLEUX CHOCOLAT CANNELLE

4 pers.   **Préparation : 10 min   Cuisson : 15 min**

> 100 g de chocolat noir + 4 carrés • 3 œufs • 60 g de beurre + 20 g pour les moules • 20 g de farine • 40 g de sucre • 1 cuil. à café de cannelle

Réalisation

Préchauffez le four à 210 °C (th. 7). Beurrez quatre petits moules individuels. Cassez le chocolat en morceaux, faites-le fondre avec le beurre au micro-ondes ou à feu très doux. Battez les œufs avec le sucre jusqu'à ce que le mélange blanchisse, puis incorporez la farine et la cannelle. Ajoutez le chocolat et le beurre.

Versez dans les moules jusqu'à la moitié, déposez un carré de chocolat, recouvrez de pâte. Enfournez et laissez cuire pendant 15 minutes. Sortez du four, démoulez et laissez tiédir avant de déguster.

MOUSSE AU CAFÉ ⏱

4 pers. **Préparation : 10 min**

60 cl de crème liquide • 3 cuil. à soupe de café soluble corsé • 3 cuil. à soupe de sucre glace • grains de café à la liqueur

Réalisation

Placez la crème au réfrigérateur plusieurs heures à l'avance. Fouettez la crème au batteur électrique dans un saladier. Quand elle commence à prendre, incorporez le café puis le sucre.

Répartissez la mousse dans quatre verres et placez au frais. Juste avant de servir, décorez de grains de café.

MOUSSE DE BANANE ⏱

4 pers.   **Préparation : 10 min**

4 bananes • 200 g de fromage blanc • 100 g de sucre
• 1 citron vert • 4 blancs d'œufs • sel

Réalisation

Pressez le citron vert. Pelez les bananes. Mixez les
bananes avec le jus de citron et le sucre. Battez les
blancs en neige avec une pincée de sel. Incorporez-les
délicatement à la crème de banane.

Répartissez la mousse dans quatre coupes et placez
au frais en attendant de servir.

PÊCHES À LA CRÈME DE CASSIS ⏱

4 pers.   **Préparation : 10 min**

4 pêches • 4 cuil. à soupe de crème de cassis • 1 branche
d'estragon

Réalisation

Pelez les pêches, émincez-les en lamelles, disposez-les
sur quatre petites assiettes et arrosez d'un filet de crème
de cassis. Parsemez de feuilles d'estragon ciselé.

PETITS GÂTEAUX AU YAOURT ET AU CITRON

4 pers. (8 gâteaux) **Préparation : 10 min** **Cuisson : 15 min**

1 yaourt nature • 2 pots de yaourt de farine • 2 pots de yaourt de sucre • 1 pot de yaourt d'amandes en poudre • 1 pot de yaourt de beurre fondu • 3 œufs • 1 sachet de levure • 1 citron non traité • sel

Réalisation

Préchauffez le four à 180 °C (th. 6). Beurrez des petits moules individuels. Videz le pot de yaourt dans un saladier, lavez-le et servez-vous-en comme instrument de mesure. Faites fondre le beurre. Râpez le zeste du citron.

Versez le sucre dans le saladier, ajoutez une pincée de sel, mélangez, puis ajoutez la farine, la levure, la poudre d'amandes, les œufs, le zeste et le beurre fondu. Fouettez pour obtenir une pâte lisse, versez dans les moules et enfournez. Laissez cuire pendant 15 minutes en surveillant la couleur. Démoulez et servez tiède avec de la confiture.

Notre conseil : faites cuire les gâteaux pendant que vous préparez les autres plats, ils tiédiront pendant le repas.

PETITS GÂTEAUX MOELLEUX AUX NOISETTES

4 pers.   **Préparation : 5 min   Cuisson : 15 min**

100 g de farine • 80 g de beurre • 80 g de sucre • 80 g de
noisettes en poudre • 2 œufs • ½ sachet de levure • 2 cuil.
à soupe de crème liquide • sel

Réalisation

Préchauffez le four à 180 °C (th. 6). Faites fondre
le beurre dans une casserole ou au micro-ondes.
Fouettez le sucre et les œufs entiers dans un saladier,
incorporez la farine, la levure, les noisettes, la crème,
une pincée de sel et le beurre fondu.
Fouettez pour obtenir une pâte lisse et versez dans
quatre petits ramequins. Enfournez et laissez cuire
pendant 12 à 15 minutes. Servez tiède ou froid.

Notre conseil : ces petits gâteaux se mangent aussi bien
au dessert avec de la compote, de la confiture, de la
glace qu'au goûter ou au petit déjeuner.

PETITS-SUISSES GLACÉS AUX FRUITS ROUGES ⏱

4 pers. **Préparation : 5 min**

8 petits-suisses • 4 cuil. à soupe de sucre • 400 g de fruits rouges frais (fraises, framboises, groseilles)

Réalisation

Fouettez les petits-suisses avec le sucre, répartissez-les dans quatre petits ramequins, déposez dessus des fruits rouges. Saupoudrez d'un peu de sucre glace juste au moment de servir.

Notre conseil : si vous utilisez des fraises, rincez-les, épongez-les, équeutez-les et coupez-les éventuellement en deux ou quatre.

POÊLÉE D'ABRICOTS, MIEL, GINGEMBRE, AMANDES ⏰

4 pers. **Préparation : 5 min** **Cuisson : 5 min**

> 1 grande boîte d'abricots au naturel • 20 g de beurre • 2 cuil. à soupe de gingembre moulu • 3 cuil. à soupe de miel • 4 cuil. à soupe d'amandes effilées

Réalisation

Égouttez les abricots. Faites chauffer le beurre dans une poêle, mettez les oreillons d'abricot, faites-les dorer légèrement, arrosez de miel, saupoudrez de gingembre, mélangez.

Faites griller les amandes à sec dans une poêle. Répartissez les abricots sur quatre assiettes, arrosez de sauce et parsemez d'amandes.

Notre conseil : accompagnez d'une boule de glace à la vanille ou au pain d'épices.

POIRES AU CHOCOLAT

4 pers. **Préparation : 10 min** **Cuisson : 3 min**

4 poires au sirop • 100 g de chocolat noir • 4 cuil. à soupe d'amandes effilées

Réalisation

Égouttez les poires, coupez-les en lamelles, disposez-les en rosace sur des petites assiettes.

Faites fondre le chocolat au micro-ondes ou au bain-marie. Versez sur les lamelles de poires. Faites griller les amandes effilées à sec dans une poêle, parsemez-les sur les assiettes.

SALADE DE FRUITS EXOTIQUES ⊕

4 pers. **Préparation : 5 min**

2 mangues • 10 litchis au sirop • 1 petite boîte d'ananas au sirop • 20 cl de jus de fruits de la passion

Réalisation

Pelez les mangues, retirez le noyau et coupez la chair en dés. Mettez-les dans un saladier, ajoutez les morceaux d'ananas et les litchis égouttés.

Arrosez de jus de fruits de la passion, mélangez, répartissez dans quatre verres ou quatre coupes et mettez au frais en attendant de servir.

TIRAMISU EXPRESS AUX FRAISES ⏲

4 pers.   **Préparation : 10 min**

> 1 paquet de biscuits roses • 250 g de mascarpone • 50 g de sucre glace • 250 g de fraises

Réalisation

Lavez, épongez les fraises, équeutez-les et mixez-les. Mélangez le mascarpone avec la moitié du sucre glace et les fraises mixées.

Répartissez les biscuits coupés en petits morceaux et la mousse aux fraises en couches superposées dans quatre verres, terminez par un nuage de sucre glace. Servez frais.

TOASTS AUX AMANDES

4 pers. **Préparation : 10 min** **Cuisson : 10 min**

4 tranches de pain brioché • 100 g d'amandes en poudre
• 60 g de sucre • 1 blanc d'œuf • 1 noisette de beurre

Réalisation

Préchauffez le four à 210 °C (th. 7). Battez le blanc d'œuf avec le sucre, puis incorporez la poudre d'amandes. Tartinez les tranches de pain brioché avec ce mélange.

Beurrez légèrement la plaque du four, déposez les tranches de pain brioché et passez au four pendant 10 minutes. Servez tiède.

VACHERIN FRAMBOISES ⏱

4 pers. **Préparation : 10 min**

½ litre de sorbet framboise • 4 meringues nature • 150 g
de framboises

Réalisation

Émiettez grossièrement les meringues. Répartissez-en la moitié dans quatre verres, déposez dessus une boule de sorbet, recouvrez de meringue et enfin de framboises fraîches. Servez aussitôt.

Nos conseils : ajoutez un peu de chantilly. Vous pouvez aussi réaliser ce dessert avec des fraises ou, en hiver, avec de la glace au chocolat ou au café.

YAOURT À LA FLEUR D'ORANGER ⏱

4 pers. **Préparation : 5 min**

4 yaourts nature • 4 cuil. à soupe d'eau de fleur d'oranger • 4 cuil. à café de cassonade • 4 zestes d'orange confite

Réalisation

Versez chaque yaourt dans un verre, ajoutez un peu d'eau de fleur d'oranger et une cuillerée à café de cassonade. Réservez au frais. Au moment de servir, coupez les zestes d'orange en petits dés et parsemez-en les yaourts.

INDEX DES RECETTES

•

Entrées express — 9

Bricks de sardines — 9

Brochettes italiennes — 10

Bruschettas au jambon et au parmesan — 11

Cabécous panés au sésame ⏲ — 12

Cappuccino de châtaignes au bacon — 13

Cassolettes d'escargots aux champignons ⏲ — 14

Céleri rémoulade et pomme verte au magret fumé — 15

Champignons crus à la coriandre ⏲ — 16

Chèvre frais, anchois et tomates confites ⏲ — 17

Concombre au cumin ⏲ — 18

Crème d'avocat au piment ⏲ — 18

Crème de thon, câpres et ciboulette ⏲ — 19

Croustillants de crevettes à la coriandre — 20

Endives et pommes au saumon ⏲ — 21

Faisselle aux oignons et aux épices ⏲ — 22

Faisselles, fenouil et poivre ⏲ — 22

Frisée, jambon, fromage et noix ⏲ — 23

Gaspacho de roquette — 24

Guacamole et surimi ⏲ — 25

Mesclun aux herbes et à l'orange ⏲ — 26

Mille-feuilles d'avocat au saumon cru — 27

Mousse de piquillos et chèvre frais ⏲ — 28

Mousse de sardines ⏲ 28

Petites terrines de thon au fromage frais ⏲ 29

Pizzettas calzone 30

Ravioles à la crème et aux herbes ⏲ 31

Salade de chou blanc aux raisins 32

Salade de Parme aux pistaches 33

Salade de pois chiches, tomates et olives 34

Salade de raie sauce gribiche 35

Salade de tomates, pois chiches et roquette au cumin ⏲ 36

Salade pomme-carottes au citron et au miel ⏲ 37

Saumon fumé, tartare pomme oignons ⏲ 38

Saumon fumé, chantilly au raifort 39

Soupe froide de courgettes à la menthe 40

Soupe glacée de tomates aux épices ⏲ 41

Soupe verte 42

Terrines de thon express ⏲ 43

Velouté d'asperges au saumon 44

Velouté de carottes au fenouil grillé ⏲ 44

Velouté de courgettes coco ciboulette 45

Verrines de saumon fumé au poivre vert 46

Viande des Grisons, melon, pistaches ⏲ 47

Œufs ultra-rapides 49

Bricks à l'œuf et au thon ⏲ 49

Œufs brouillés, copeaux de parmesan ⏲ 50

Œufs cocotte, pistou, tomates confites et croûtons 51
Œufs cocotte, tomate et chorizo 52
Œufs mayonnaise au cumin 53
Œufs mollets, épinards frais 54
Œufs mollets et mouillettes d'asperges 55
Omelette chèvre-estragon ⏰ 56
Omelette herbes et fromage 57

Poissons et crustacés minute **59**
Cabillaud à la choucroute 59
Cabillaud vapeur au curry 60
Crevettes sautées aux légumes 61
Gambas à la coriandre 62
Haddock en salade à l'orange 63
Haddock et chou chinois en salade ⏰ 64
Lotte à la pancetta et aux câpres 65
Lotte au curry 66
Mijotée de poissons express 67
Moules au thym 68
Pavés de lieu coco curry à la coriandre 69
Petits calamars grillés 69
Rougets au bacon 70
Rougets tomates et tapenade 71
Saint-Jacques aux herbes et au parmesan 72
Saint-Jacques poêlées aux échalotes 73

Salade de haricots verts au crabe 74

Salade de lentilles au thon ⏲ 75

Salade de mâche et de thon à l'ananas 76

Salade de mâche, saumon et baies roses ⏲ 77

Salade de poissons fumés à l'oignon rouge 78

Salade de mangues, roquette et crevettes 79

Saumon grillé et pousses d'épinard 80

Saumon pané aux herbes 81

Tagliatelles au saumon, curry et coriandre 82

Tagliatelles aux crevettes 83

Tagliatelles aux gambas 84

Tartare de saumon au gingembre 85

Viandes et volailles rapides **87**

Aiguillettes de canard au poivre vert 87

Aiguillettes de canard miel et noix 88

Aiguillettes de poulet au curry 89

Bavette aux échalotes 90

Bœuf aux légumes croquants à la coriandre 91

Bœuf aux oignons et au gingembre 92

Bœuf sauté au gingembre 93

Bricks de bœuf aux épices 94

Canard au curry 95

Cuisses de canard confit grillées aux lentilles 96

Émincé d'agneau au basilic ⏲ 97

Émincé de bœuf au paprika 98
Émincé de bœuf, salade de roquette 99
Escalopes de dinde aux tomates confites 100
Escalopes de poulet au parmesan 101
Escalopes de veau gratinées 102
Faux filet à la thaïe 103
Foie de veau, caramel au citron 104
Fricassée de poulet aux fruits secs 105
Grillades de gigot d'agneau à la fleur de thym ⏲ 106
Jambon au poivre ⏲ 107
Lamelles de porc à l'ananas 108
Hachis de bœuf pimenté au basilic ⏲ 109
Pâtes fraîches à la sauge, coppa grillée 110
Pavés de bœuf, crème de baies roses 111
Petits pilons de poulet au miel 111
Poulet au sésame 112
Poulet aux nouilles chinoises 113
Poulet coco coriandre 114
Poulet crème estragon 115
Poulet tandoori, riz basmati 116
Rôti de magrets à l'orange et au miel 117
Salade alsacienne 118
Salade d'endives, jambon, roquefort et noix ⏲ 119
Salade de magrets de canard aux marrons 120
Tartare aller-retour aux herbes ⏲ 121

Tartare classique ⏲ 122
Tartare thaï ⏲ 123

Desserts vite prêts **125**
Ananas sauté à la menthe 125
Bananes coco rhum 126
Bouchées sablées aux framboises ⏲ 127
Chantilly orange cacao ⏲ 127
Compote de cerises aux amandes 128
Compote de fruits rouges 129
Crème au chocolat et pralin 130
Crème de marrons au chocolat ⏲ 131
Crumbles express aux pommes 132
Figues à la brousse, miel et cannelle ⏲ 133
Figues rôties au caramel salé 133
Figues sèches pochées au miel, glace vanille 134
Framboises, mousse de fromage blanc et biscuits roses ⏲ 135
Gâteau au chocolat TGV 136
Glace en robe ⏲ 137
Litchis à la rose ⏲ 137
Moelleux chocolat cannelle 138
Mousse au café ⏲ 139
Mousse de banane ⏲ 140
Pêches à la crème de cassis ⏲ 140
Petits gâteaux au yaourt et au citron 141

Petits gâteaux moelleux aux noisettes   142

Petits-suisses glacés aux fruits rouges ⏲   143

Poêlée d'abricots, miel, gingembre, amandes ⏲   144

Poires au chocolat   145

Salade de fruits exotiques ⏲   145

Tiramisu express aux fraises ⏲   146

Toasts aux amandes   147

Vacherin framboises ⏲   147

Yaourt à la fleur d'oranger ⏲   148

VOUS AVEZ AIMÉ CE LIVRE?

Vous trouverez également dans la même collection

LES TITRES CUISINE

Recettes express • Tartes salées et sucrées • Pâtes • Recettes éco • Crêpes salées et sucrées • Crumbles • Soupes • Recettes pour débutants • Recettes aux œufs • Tartares et carpaccios • Wok • Quiches, tartes et tatins • Gratins • Fêtes et fiestas • Tout chocolat • Cakes salés et sucrés • Recettes pour deux • Desserts simplissimes • Recettes végétariennes • Recettes provençales • Recettes du Pays basque • Recettes d'Italie • Recettes du Maroc • Recettes juives • Salades express • Confitures, gelées et marmelades • Brochettes et barbecue • Recettes de grand-mère • Recettes d'Espagne • Recettes d'Asie • Recettes du congélo • Recettes alsaciennes • Recettes lyonnaises • Dîners à thèmes • Petits et grands gâteaux • Hachis et farcis • Assiettes gourmandes • Cookies, muffins & Co • Fondues, raclettes et pierrades • Goûters d'enfant • Pains et brioches • Plats mijotés • Recettes solo • Recettes latino • Recettes 10 minutes chrono • Riz et risottos • Recettes créoles • Petits plats aux champignons • Recettes pour débutants n°2 • Purées et mousselines • Papillotes et bricks • Sauces salées et sucrées • Recettes à moins de 2 euros ! • Cuisine de l'étudiant • Plats canailles • Petits plats de la Méditerranée • Recettes sur le pouce • Les Grandes Salades • Yaourts et douceurs de lait • Recettes au micro-ondes • Poissons et fruits de mer • Cuisine de bistrot • Recettes des amoureux • Machine à pain • Pot-au-feu, potées et Cie • Recettes SOS porte-monnaie en détresse • Tutti Smoothies • Plancha et barbecue • Verrines de tous les jours • Salades fraîches • Tapas & dips • Glaces, sorbets & co • Verrines du soleil • Dîners improvisés • 100 % tajines • Mini et maxi cocottes • Les meilleures recettes classiques • Soupes des 4 saisons • Terrines, pâtés & cie • Cuillères, verrines et mises en bouche • Des amis à dîner • Pâtes, nouilles et cie • Cuisine à la vapeur • Recettes et menus à prix mini • Crumbles, tartes et clafoutis • Cuisine de la mer • Papillotes gourmandes

LES TITRES CUISINE / SANTÉ

Recettes pour bébé • Recettes pour diabétiques • Recettes Oméga 3 • Fibrissime • Recettes vapeur et minceur • Menus minceur • Recettes minceur épices et aromates • Recettes anti-âge • Recettes anti-cholestérol • Soupes santé et minceur • Menus pour futures mamans • Desserts minceur • Recettes minceur d'ici et d'ailleurs • Les meilleurs recettes du régime crétois • Recettes à faible IG • Recettes anti-allergies • Recettes anti-stress • Le petit livre de la minceur • Le Décodeur minceur • Verrines minceur • Recettes contre le cancer • 5 fruits et légumes par jour • Recettes minceur pour mon homme • Agar-agar, secrets et recettes • Recettes légères au Wok • Menus et recettes minceur • Recettes pour un corps de rêve

Pour être informé en permanence sur notre catalogue et les dernières nouveautés publiées dans cette collection, consultez notre site internet www.editionsfirst.fr

Dans la collection **Le petit livre de**
vous trouverez également **les thématiques**
suivantes :

Le petit livre de Cuisine ●●●●●●

Le petit livre de Culture générale ●●●●●●

Le petit livre de Insolites ●●●●●●

Le petit livre de Tourisme ●●●●●●

Le petit livre de Langues ●●●●●●

Le petit livre de Humour ●●●●●●

Pour consulter notre catalogue et
découvrir les dernières nouveautés,

rendez-vous sur **www.editionsfirst.com** !